What People are

Saying about

Train Ride to Heaven ...

Glen Maholovich was a pillar in his rural community along the Alabama-Florida panhandle border. Energetic, skilled with his hands, and with a kind heart as big as all outdoors, Glen was invariably one of the first to lend a hand to anyone in need. Then, in the prime of his life Glen is stricken by Amyotrophic Lateral Sclerosis (ALS) a fatal disease better known as Lou Gehrig's Disease. *Train Ride to Heaven: Memoir of a Family's Love* by Vanessa Maholovich as told to Sherry Sapp is a heart-rending but inspiring memoir of how Glen Maholovich's condition draws his family and community together and of his spiritual triumph over fatally debilitating adversity.

~ Dwight Jon Zimmerman, #1 *New York Times* bestselling author

This book is filled with commitment, love and strong faith. Even facing this terminal disease, Glen uses humor to help his family cope while his wife, family and friends provide love and strength that comes from within and from God. The challenges this family faced will be such an encouragement to others as they read this very touching book.

~ Deborah M. Miles, RN, LCSW, author of *The Power Within: Claim It!*

Train Ride to Heaven details an inspiring journey of one family's faith, love, and determination to help their husband/father transcend the ravages of a debilitating, fatal disease while maintaining his precious self-identity. For seven years, they did so with dignity, respect, and compassion. A must read!

~ Bonnie Bartel Latino Co-author, *Your Gift to Me*

TRAIN RIDE
TO
HEAVEN

BY

VANESSA
MAHOLOVICH
AS TOLD TO
SHERRY SAPP

Red Engine Press
Pittsburgh, PA

Library of Congress Control Number: 2015952624

ISBN: 978-1-943267-02-6 Trade Paperback

Cover photo by Leonard Hursh of Atmore, AL
Photo first published by Sherry Digmon and Myrna Monroe co-owners and co-publishers of Grace Publishing Company as a cover of "atmore" magazine

"I Hope You Dance"
Music and Lyrics by Mark D. Sanders and Tia Sillers
Copyright (c) 2000, Uni/MCA Nashville

Red Engine Press
Bridgeville, PA

Cover design and layout by Joyce Faulkner

Printed in the United States.

Contents

Contents (Continued)

Contents (Continued)

For My Grandfather, Joseph Glen, Who, in the '70s . . .

For my grandfather who in the early '70s
Was rockin' the Afro
Showing off his bell-bottom jeans
And his polyester shirt
Wearin' his favorite platform shoes,
Friday nights could be found
Tearing up the dirt roads in his
Green '68 Ford Mustang
Honking at all the girls as he rolled by
It was all about being a ladies man.

For my grandfather, who in the mid '70s,
Could be found on the baseball field
Pitching a no-hitter and setting school records
Athletics was his favorite thing to do
He wasn't known for studying or having good grades
But he still found a way to pass
Graduating high school was one of the most
Exciting times of his life.
After high school, he started to begin his
Adult life with a very special lady.

For my grandfather in the late '70s
He could be found
Heading to the chapel to meet his bride
Making home improvements to his new house
Going to church on Sunday
Eating Sunday Dinner with his family
Or being with his family during the week
Preparing for a new arrival.
It was all about his wife and his brand new baby girl.

By Zachary Maholovich, 14,
Based on stories told to him by his Grandfather, "Bo"

PROLOGUE

Glen Maholovich was 54 when he died a prisoner in his own body, dependent on round-the-clock care by family and friends. He died of Lou Gehrig's disease in 2011. He was just one of the thousands of people every year who die of debilitating terminal diseases.

We hear about the struggles of celebrities who acquire terrible diseases. Our hearts break for them. Their futures were so promising. We follow their plights with rapt attention, reaching out with get-well cards, teddy bears and prayers. We wonder silently how on earth they make it through the day under such crushing misfortune. We thank God that we aren't in their shoes.

Glen was not a celebrity. He was not a titan of industry or a professional ballplayer. He wasn't wealthy. His was not a household name, nor was he in any way remarkable in the way that attracts newspapers. He was as ordinary a guy as you'd ever meet. Glen was plain vanilla ice cream. Maholovich, pronounced Ma-HOHL-oh-vich, is Yugoslavian and rare. His grandchildren called him Bo, the only pronunciation the grandchildren could manage for the Slavic endearment for "grandfather."

Glen was little known outside our tiny Southern Alabama community, but he meant the entire world to us. He would never have thought so himself, but he was truly — all the way through to the marrow of his bones — a good man. Not a flawless man, but a truly good man. Glen was one of those people who lived for his friends and family. He was content with all that he had and wanted nothing more — except a little more time.

The loss of a genuinely good man burns a hole through his survivors' souls with white-hot intensity, if only because the presence of that person seems as necessary to their existence as the air they breathe or the food they eat. That is how it was for us.

Celebrities with terminal debilitating illnesses are the exception, not the rule. Glen's life, his affliction and his death were like those of the thousands upon thousands of other ordinary people who battle fatal, crippling illnesses. Like Glen, the overwhelming majority of such patients are workaday people, living typical lives in their own neighborhoods and hometowns.

The average person struggles with disabling ailments day in and day out, without financial resources, without famous friends, and without a fan base or a staff of employees. I do not mean in any way to diminish the agony and heartache of celebrities and their families. I mean only to instill a measure of encouragement, hope and comfort to other ordinary families who have more limited resources, by telling the story of one of them.

This is the story of Glen, his life and the courage he displayed when the use of his body was gone.

But this isn't only Glen's story. It is also the story of the people around him. This is the story of a family, their friends and their community and how the lives of people who love someone so stricken are radically changed. Like it or not, a debilitating illness dictates the courses of many lives.

All of us who loved Glen and lived through his disease with him were compelled to unearth our better selves in order to cope. Glen's faith, humor and courage helped show us how. We discovered, within ourselves, surprising reserves of strength and resilience we had no idea could exist.

Yet we are an ordinary family. Glen was an ordinary man. I hope that Glen's story will prove that if one ordinary family could persevere under such circumstances, so can other families. That is my fervent hope. But even if only a single family, if only a single person is helped, this story will have achieved its purpose.

And that would please Glen so very much.

PART ONE

TRAIN STATION

CHAPTER ONE

GLEN MAHOLOVICH

By the time Glen died, he had known for some time that his death was imminent. For the seven years between Christmas 2004 — when doctors diagnosed his Lou Gehrig's disease — and his death in 2011, all of us around him had known it, too.

Glen's intelligence, compassion, wit and extremely quirky view of the world were thoroughly intact when he died, although he had not been able to speak for a long time. He died completely dependent on the constant care of compassionate family, friends and professionals.

He died peacefully at home, a prisoner in his own body, two days before Thanksgiving. Word of his death spread quickly. Almost immediately, his bedroom filled with people who loved him, while others spilled into the hallway waiting to say goodbye. The fact was that in the last months of his life, the small cottage had been filled with people most of the time.

Glen had been unable to communicate except with his eyes and a few indecipherable guttural sounds. Before he grew too exhausted to do so, he had typed, with his toe, what he wanted to say into an electronic voice-simulating device.

Amyotrophic Lateral Sclerosis, often called Lou Gehrig's disease, is mysterious, debilitating and fatal. No one knows how it is acquired, who will acquire it, or how to treat or cure it.

Joseph Glen Maholovich was an amiable, optimistic man who lived his entire life in one of those tiny rural towns that we pass through on the highway on our way to somewhere else.

My name is Vanessa Maholovich, and sometime during the year 2000, my 45-year-old husband became one of the infinitesimally small number of people in the world to contract ALS. It would take another interminable four years for us to know what was causing his baffling array of bizarre symptoms.

At the same time everyone else adjusted to living in a brand new century, our own world was disintegrating. But it happened so slowly that we never saw it coming. In the same way that a child doesn't feel himself growing taller, our lives began to crumble, stealthily, just outside our consciousness. It isn't that way for all ALS patients, some of whom experience symptoms rapidly over a short period. That is just how it was for Glen.

Before Glen got sick, he was a muscular, six-feet-tall, 225-pound genial bear of a man. I, on the other hand, am petite, a fact that later posed some difficulties as his illness progressed. Glen was Marlboro-Man handsome and naturally gifted at all things physical. In school, he had been a star baseball and football player and remained compulsively athletic until he became ill.

"He could pitch a baseball with enough force to split a board. We never saw anyone with an arm as strong as that," said Ronnie Berry, Glen's brother-in-law. The two of them were like brothers.

Eventually Glen had greater acceptance of his disease than those of us who loved him. He referred to his illness as his "cross to bear." He did not feel a bit sorry for himself. That was his way of saying that everyone on earth suffers personal hardships. Lou Gehrig's disease just happened to be the one assigned to him.

Terrible diseases afflict people in every walk of life. They happen without warning and strike exactly the same way that rain falls on the just and the unjust alike. Fair or not, a fatal, debilitating disease is heartless and cruel.

Glen rarely spoke specifically of death during his illness. He was an unapologetic optimist. But when he did, he spoke as if life for everyone is lived aboard a splendid passenger train. Glen described his, and everyone's, death as the end of a railway journey pulling at last into its final station at heaven. According to Glen's vision, everyone on earth rode this heaven-bound train. But each person's journey was individual, unique and surprising. Travelers took slightly different routes at slightly different times and sometimes at different speeds. They spent time with other travelers for a while, then perhaps switched seats for different views, and journeyed on. No traveler ever knew when his or her particular car would arrive at the station, just that it would.

Sometimes a traveler's car might arrive at the station a great deal earlier than his loved ones aboard later cars, but that just meant he would be the one to welcome each of them as they rolled into the station. That was the case with him, he said.

Sometimes Glen talked about the people he loved who had boarded the train long before he did. They would be waiting for him at the station and he would be happy to see them again.

Glen repeatedly told us all that he would be waiting for each one of us when we arrived at the station, but still he charged me to make sure everyone actually boarded the train. "Make sure they all come," he said again and again.

ALS is death by gradual paralysis, culminating in the loss of most bodily functions, including swallowing, speaking and raising one's head. The strength and control of muscles are lost, but not the nerves that feel heat, cold, pain or pressure. The patient is still able to see, smell, taste, hear, and experience touch. Lou Gehrig's disease is not in itself painful, but ALS patients can feel an itchy nose or the pain of a stubbed toe exactly as anyone else would. He can smell fried chicken cooking or his granddaughter's strawberry shampoo. Glen's thinking was as sharp as ever to his last breath and his sense of humor remained intact.

I use the word "he" for convenience, even though a slightly smaller percentage of ALS patients are women. ALS strikes generally between the ages of forty and seventy, although children have been stricken. The disease does not show any preference for race, ethnicity, education, geography, income, lifestyle, family history or previous condition of health. The disease occurs as randomly as a lightning strike.

A diagnosis of ALS is a death sentence. So far, there is no cure or treatment. Although it means certain death for the afflicted, ALS, like many other debilitating diseases, doesn't stop there. The disease takes over and changes the lives of others who love the patient. Glen's disease affected the lives of our children, our grandchildren and our friends.

For me, the idea that Glen Maholovich — whose very identity was so intertwined with his physical ability and who prided himself on his self-sufficiency — would become utterly dependent on others, would have been incomprehensible to me before his illness. However, when he got sick, it was like watching a superhero drained of all strength, rendering him helpless as a kitten. He became Superman exposed to Kryptonite or Samson after Delilah cut off his hair.

Lou Gehrig's disease stole Glen's most outwardly identifiable attributes — his strength, dexterity and self-reliance. He relied on these abilities to be a good husband, father, neighbor and friend. Those abilities served him, and the rest of us,well. He never did realize that his qualities of spirituality, kindness, love and wisdom remained lit candles in the dark long after the physical abilities were gone.

For the two of us, the diagnosis of ALS marked the end of all of our plans and dreams. It was the end of everything familiar and routine. Life flipped over on its head and none of the old rules applied. We were turtles on our backs.

When we learned of the diagnosis, it was as if we had been happily traveling a well-trodden path toward a much-anticipated destination. We had been traveling this comfortable path for years with just a bump or a pothole now and then, but no great chasms.

Out of the blue, we found ourselves face-to-face with an impassable wall of granite. It reached to the sky and extended around the world. There was no way to climb it, no way to tunnel under it and no way to go around it. The wall had appeared out of nowhere and our road — the only road we knew — was closed.

By that, I don't mean that our road was closed for a little while for repairs or inclement weather. It was closed for good. There was no "will reopen at . . ." sign.

We realized that we were never going to travel to our destination by this path. Almost immediately, we learned we could not reach our destination by any road at all. The wall had imposed upon us an entirely new and most unpleasant destination. We did not choose it and we did not want it.

That didn't matter; we could dislike it all we wanted. We could rant and curse the stars, but there was no changing it. Like it or not, we had to travel a different and distinctly unpleasant path, toward a place that we had no wish to go. We had to travel the new path without preparation, experience, or any frame of reference. We had no trail guide, no map, not even a compass to help us navigate this path. The path itself provided precious few directional signs. We had entered foreign terrain that imposed a steep and merciless learning curve.

FAMILY PHOTO 1998

CHAPTER TWO

HE WAS MY LIFELONG
SOUL MATE

Glen's life and mine had been inextricably bound together for so
many years that a life without him seemed inconceivable. We
were a couple from the time we were both fourteen-year-old
high-school sophomores. By the time he died, we were both still
relatively young, but we had been together for forty years. We were
married for thirty-six of those years.

There may have been brief intervals as teenagers where we weren't
a couple, but we came back together, magnetically drawn by
a powerful spiritual bond.

Glen and I grew up in the best possible years to grow up, in a wonderful
rural community, inhabited by good people.

I grew up in Walnut Hill, Escambia County, Florida, a tiny rural
community just south of the Alabama-Florida state line. Glen lived
just a few miles down the road in Bratt, Florida, which is termed a
"populated area," because it isn't officially incorporated.

Glen's house fronted twenty-odd acres and was situated on the Florida
side of the Florida-Alabama state line. The people across the road
from Glen lived in Alabama. After we were married, we lived in that
house for many years.

The nearest large town is Atmore, Alabama, where I live now. "Large"
is a relative term because Atmore had only 2,100 households in 1971
when Glen and I met. Now it has about 3,100 households. To us it
was large. As young people, we referred to Atmore as "downtown."

Atmore has a couple of small local newspapers that publish three days a week. The news is thoroughly local with a decidedly Southern flavor. The area is rural with a farming and timber-based economy. At one time, it was the home of a large Vanity Fair lingerie factory, which closed down some time back. There is a YMCA, a nine-hole golf course and a city-operated recreation program. There is one public high school with about 535 students in all, a 49-bed hospital, a public airport for single-engine airplanes and seventy-two churches. The Wind Creek Casino is just off the highway.

The disadvantage of living in a small town is that medical resources are fewer than there would be in a large city. The advantage is that you know your neighbors. In fact, you come to know almost everyone. That small-town closeness may have worked to our advantage in terms of the support we received from family, friends and even strangers throughout Glen's illness.

Our community was small, and we were as country as cornbread, but we were educated, savvy, innovative and hardworking. Those were the Andy Griffith years, during the fifties, sixties and seventies. We walked everywhere on unpaved roads. We wandered off to go swimming without telling anyone, all the while completely confident that we were safe.

Glen and I met in 1971, when a new car cost $1,275 and a new house cost roughly $25,000—about as much as the down payment for a house the year Glen died. A gallon of gas cost 40 cents, a movie ticket $1.50 and a postage stamp eight cents. The minimum wage was $1.60 an hour. Telephones were attached to walls. Never did we dream we would someday use "wireless communication devices," such as the ones we saw on TV science-fiction programs. The words microwave, CD, digital, video, download, and streaming were either foreign to us or had entirely different meanings. Richard Nixon was president of the United States, George C. Wallace was governor of Alabama and Reuben Askew was governor of Florida. The Vietnam War was still going. But we were fourteen years old and family, church, school and outdoor activities were the center of our lives.

Glen was smart, imaginative, innovative and funny. He became class president, not because he sought the limelight but because he was a genuinely likable guy for whom no one had a harsh word. Even his two older sisters insist that Glen was such a good-natured child, they cannot remember ever having a single cross word with him.

He liked people, all people, rich or poor, smart or not, pretty or not. He saw people's hearts, rather than their exterior. His sense of humor was so well honed that he had a subconscious impulse to transform any tale of some unpleasantness into something so hysterically funny there was nothing to do but laugh. He used that humor often when he was sick.

WEDDING PICTURE, 1975

CHAPTER THREE

NICE GUY, BUT NOT PERFECT

Before I go too far, I must make it clear that Glen was no saint. Glen had his faults. He was strong-willed. He was a workaholic and he was stubborn. He was an exasperating perfectionist with regard to his work. He multi-tasked in maddeningly disorganized ways. He often started a new project before finishing the old one. He sometimes forgot that other people — myself, for example — did not have the physical strength or natural ability that he had. I called him "the golden child" because nothing was ever hard for him. He had many natural gifts that he took in stride as if they were nothing special. But if you weren't doing a thing — something with which he had great expertise — the way he thought it should be done, he let you know about it. He was not harsh or condescending, just very determined that if a thing was going to be done at all; it should be done correctly and with precision. The whole family learned not to wear our feelings on our sleeves.

He was physically fit; but still he ate way too much, way too fast. He loved steak. A lot. And he could eat ice cream literally by the plateful. He could be a jokester at times. More than anything, he loved to laugh and he loved to make other people laugh. He was very good at it.

That would not normally be a shortcoming, but when he became ill and laughed uproariously when he suffered dangerous falls, I was both frightened and infuriated. I did not find that one bit funny!

And finally, he was a tightwad so notorious that everyone who knew him openly joked about it. He insisted on squeezing the very last penny's worth of value from every dollar he ever spent. Even when we were teenagers, he would make and take extra sandwiches to school to sell them for outrageous sums of money. And he was a serious businessman. You didn't get that sandwich until he had the cash in his hand.

If he could fabricate or build a thing otherwise sold in stores — and he nearly always could — he did. If something was old, but still functional, he saw no sense in replacing it. Devising ingenious solutions to all manner of problematic situations was second nature to him, and he thrived on it. He would have been a good engineer. Even when a thing could be done more conveniently by paying professionals, Glen still did it himself.

None of us has ever been able to figure out the source of that particular idiosyncrasy. But he genuinely detested spending money. If he did spend an amount that he considered too much, we never heard the end of it. We all remember the time when Glen spent what he considered an exorbitant amount of money for a cruise, then took every opportunity for months afterward to complain about that outrageous expense.

He was always frugal. After his death, we ran across something that he had written for me to find. It was a list for me having to do with money matters.

Glen had a modest upbringing, like we all did, but not a deprived one. No one really knows why he was so concerned about saving. Maybe it was cultural. His Yugoslavian ancestors had made their way to Alabama, where they worked as sharecroppers before acquiring land of their own. We don't know if they were obsessed with thrift, but we do know they had a very strong work ethic, which clearly found its way into Glen's genes.

For most all his life when he wasn't working . . . he was still working. Every summer as boys, Glen and his cousin helped his great uncle, who farmed 80-100 acres. Glen drove the tractor. Both of them baled hay and loaded the hay bales onto a truck just as soon as they were big enough to do it.

As soon as the boys were through, they'd run off and go swimming in the creek. When the boys were older, the pair rode all over the countryside in Glen's old hand-crank-starter jeep.

It didn't change when Glen grew up. He worked as a bank collections officer during the day, but on his own time, he landscaped the grounds for the bank. When he wasn't doing that, he stayed busy remodeling rooms and houses and built furniture, among other things. All of these were skills were self taught.

CHAPTER FOUR

PECULIAR SYMPTOMS

A t age forty-five, we started thinking about retirement. In twenty years, Glen would retire from the First National Bank and Trust in Atmore where he worked as a collections officer and I would retire from nursing. We had half-made plans to take a cruise to Alaska for our thirty-fifth wedding anniversary. Later, we would travel to other places. We would enjoy our family, play with our grandchildren, and move to someplace near the water. We both loved the water. There was no particular rush to finalize those plans, because retirement was years away.

Or so we thought.

Sometime in 2001, at about the time of the 9-11 World Trade Center and Pentagon terrorist attacks, Glen began to notice occasional, peculiar symptoms. The symptoms were indistinct, and they were not the symptoms of any common illness we knew. They were infrequent and not terribly pronounced. In the beginning, these strange symptoms simply baffled and annoyed us.

As time went on, they became more puzzling. For the next few years, Glen experienced slurred speech, difficulty in swallowing, spontaneous and uncontrollable muscle twitching, and an inexplicable difficulty in controlling the movement of his tongue. He told me he was having trouble making his mouth produce certain syllables. Sometimes he choked.

An increasing weakness and fatigue were among the most pronounced symptoms. Before, Glen had been almost tireless. He thrived on outdoor physical activities and loved working with his hands. Slowly, he changed from a man accustomed to long hours of hard physical activity at work and play to a man who became exhausted and worn out with the slightest exertion. He began experiencing muscle cramps and his body ached, particularly his arms. His powerful muscles became inexplicably weak. He suffered neck pain, headaches, and strange fevers.

At times, the muscles in his upper arms twitched so uncontrollably I had trouble sleeping next to him. He began to have difficulty moving his arms and hands. Alarming signs of muscular atrophy began to appear between the thumb and forefinger of both of his hands.

Sometimes he rubbed his arms and told me, "Vanessa, I don't know what is going on, but there is something wrong with me. Something isn't right. I can just feel it."

For the most part, the symptoms were not obvious to others, and for quite some time our friends had no idea anything was wrong. It was easy to attribute the symptoms to ordinary things like overwork, lack of sleep or the beginning of some common illness. And for a long time, that's what we believed.

Eventually, his symptoms became too bizarre and happened too often for any of those reasons to make sense. And then, for no reason that anyone could understand, he began to exhibit bizarre and inappropriate emotional responses. For example, he wept when something was funny, or he laughed when something was tragic.

That began to interfere with his work. As a bank collections officer, he often had to make court appearances. His mismatched emotional outbursts interfered with his ability to do his job. He might be talking about foreclosing on someone's property and suddenly start laughing. That wasn't Glen at all. For one thing, outbursts of strong emotion were completely out of character. He was a typical male of his generation, one of those guys who kept his feelings and his emotions mostly to himself.

Even if he had been more outwardly emotional, he never would have found someone's misfortune to be humorous. His emotion in that circumstance would be sorrow, not laughter.

On the other hand, sometimes he went the opposite direction. He started to cry for no apparent reason. Sometimes he would cry when he was amused.

I wondered, "Why the heck is he crying all the time?"

As a long-time nurse, I had a fair understanding of common ailments, but this situation baffled me. I could not figure out what was wrong with him. Neither could he. Four years went by before we learned that such inappropriate emotional outbursts are typical of ALS patients. It is called the pseudobulbar affect, and is a kind of neurological disconnect. Over time, as his condition deteriorated, he lost most of his ability to express himself in a way that people could understand.

Because of the disease, Glen was forced to retire twenty years prematurely, on June 24, 2005. That was about six months after his diagnosis. But that diagnosis came only after four frustrating years of enduring inexplicable symptoms and a wearying series of visits to doctors and undergoing many tests.

Later on, long after his diagnosis, Glen wrote an email to members of his church — First Assembly of God in Atmore — reflecting on what had been happening to him during this period. He typed the email with his toe on a specially adapted keyboard:

I have been blessed all my life to be very healthy. I was a big child and teenager, you know, one of those boys with muscles and no brains. I think that is why Vanessa married me. She thought that boy is going to need help. Think of it, I have been healthy all my life. I now turn 45 and my left hand begins to not work right. It will not turn from palm down to palm up the way it should.

A few years before, I had torn some ligaments toting a door — remember muscle, no brain. I went to a doctor and he said that torn tendons would not cause that. That was the beginning of a long frustrating two years.

Every new symptom I developed, I went to a doctor who dealt with that kind of symptom. Next came neck aches, headaches and fever. Then both arms started to get a little weak. If I exerted energy by working, my whole body would cramp. I don't know how many nights I would be sound asleep and a leg cramp would hit and I would be up for a while trying to get it to ease off."

GLEN IN HIS PRIME- 41 YEARS OLD

CHAPTER FIVE

WHAT IS ALS?

Most people outside the medical community know little about ALS, except that Lou Gehrig, the famous New York Yankees baseball player for whom the disease is now called, had it. Anyone who has seen the movie *The Pride of the Yankees* knows the basic story. The gifted ballplayer was forced to retire young because of the disease. He died a couple of years later.

People generally know that ALS is bad, but not much more than that. It is not familiar because it is rare. When Glen first heard that he had ALS, he had little reaction. He had no idea what that meant.

ALS is classified as an orphan disease, which means that it has been largely overlooked by the pharmaceutical industry because it is too rare to provide the necessary financial incentive to research, produce, and market medications to treat or prevent it. The 1983 federal Orphan Drug Act was implemented to provide status and tax incentives to encourage more research and development. This has met with limited success.

A disease is considered rare, or an orphan disease, by United States National Institutes of Health criteria if it affects fewer than 200,000 people in the United States. No more than 20,000 to 30,000 people in the United States have ALS at any given time. There are nearly 314 million people, so the number of cases is very small.

As it turned out, Glen was part of an even smaller number. His type of ALS, known as Bulbar Onset ALS, is uncommon even for patients who have ALS. Ordinarily symptoms begin at the bottom of the body, in the feet and legs and move upward. Bulbar Onset ALS begins at the top of the body — the head, arms, hands, chest — and moves down. Only one in four cases of ALS is Bulbar Onset.

The consequence of such small numbers of cases means that until fairly recently there had been little substantial research accomplished. What had been done had yielded few answers, only certain confusing clues.

Lou Gehrig's disease, in simplest terms, is the death of the brain's ability to deliver messages to muscles to cause them to operate in the manner necessary to perform an ordinary function, such as scratching your ear, swallowing food or opening a door. Receiving no instructions, the muscles do nothing. After a long enough time, the unused muscles weaken, atrophy, and begin to display very fine twitches called fasciculation.

Certain parts of the body still operate as usual. The senses are unaffected, so patients can still see, feel, hear, taste and smell as they always could. The intellect remains intact. For most people, muscles of the eyes and bladder are not affected, so they function as before.

Why certain people acquire ALS remains a mystery. There is a slight indication of a genetic component, which is being studied more. But fewer than 10 percent of ALS patients have any family history of ALS. It is classified as primarily a sporadic disease. That means it could strike anyone, without regard to race, gender, nationality, geography, upbringing or lifestyle. To date, no one has any clear idea what triggers it, although there is a growing belief that a genetic predisposition combined with environmental factors may be involved. Its symptoms are oddly similar to those of Lyme disease.

Research has been picking up in recent years. One small federal study found that the relative risk of dying from ALS for military combat veterans is 1.5 times that compared to men who did not serve. The increased risk was found to exist for veterans of World War II, the Korean War, and the war in Vietnam. A different study found that the rate of ALS in young Gulf War veterans was more than two times greater than expected for the general population. So far, there are no conclusive answers.

The Veterans Administration, along with the Department of Defense, conducted studies of ALS among Gulf War veterans. The study included all 2.5 million Gulf War veterans. Investigators found that among that group, the rate of disease was double that of the general population. Because there was no real explanation for why this would be, the VA established a database for tracking. After its closure in 2011, a new one administered by the Centers for Disease Control and Prevention opened. It is not limited to veterans, but does track military service of patients within the database. (For more information, go to www.cdc.gov/als.)

Researchers from the National Institute for Occupational Safety and Health in Cincinnati wrote in the September 2012 journal Neurology that professional football players were found to have a higher propensity to contract ALS and Alzheimer's disease. Scientists gathered data on 3,439 ex-professional football players who had played at least five seasons. They discovered that the football players had triple the risk of death caused by diseases that destroy or damage brain cells and a four times greater risk of dying from ALS or Alzheimer's disease than the general population.

For the time being, no one has any idea how those numbers factor into the overall understanding of ALS, or how that might help patients. For now, these are intriguing findings, but still provide no conclusive answers.

For many patients, like Yankees ballplayer Lou Gehrig, death comes rapidly, within two to three years. That is the typical outlook. For a rare few, like world-renowned physicist Stephen Hawking, death is forestalled a great many years.

Glen's death stretched out over seven years, with a five-year period during which the illness stalled — only to return with a greater vengeance.

CHAPTER SIX

BOBBY

Glen came into my life in the ninth grade by way of my "surrogate brother," Bobby. Robert "Bobby" Lee Hudson is congenial, outspoken, witty and colorful. He is an old-fashioned gentleman of the type who will stand when a woman enters and not sit down until she sits down. He is a twenty-first century blond-haired, blue-eyed, rough-and-tumble-looking cowboy, with a more defined wild streak to his personality than Glen ever had. Glen was mellow, more even-tempered. Glen's wild side was subtle and not readily apparent. Bobby Hudson and Glen were like thunder and lightning. "I'm the guy that stands in the center of the tornado and watches everything spin around," Bobby said. Glen was the guy who stayed calm and helped other people to stay calm.

Bobby and I started school together. In our town, we moved through our single-building school, like a school of fish, from one grade to the next. We began school at one end of the building and finished at the other end. I thought all schools were like that. We started out with 70-plus pupils in our graduating class. That was more students than the school had ever seen in a single class.

Bobby had no sisters and my half-brothers did not live with us, so our relationship morphed into a sibling relationship. Bobby became protective of me.

Glen came on the scene later. He was part of the so-called "Bratt Invasion." Glen came into our lives when our school and the school in Bratt merged. Bobby and Glen both played on the school's football team. When Glen asked Bobby for an introduction to me, Bobby decided he should get to know Glen better first.

The two boys had some common interests. It turned out that Glen was extremely mechanical, as was Bobby. So they got to know each other on that basis in the beginning. Glen and Bobby shared other hobbies, including building, cars, and football, which naturally drew them together. But their lifelong friendship was cemented by a single football-related incident.

During a game, one of the players from the other team went up to Bobby and kicked him in the mouth. "The next thing I knew I was spitting out metal and blood," Bobby said. He managed to hobble over to the sidelines.

Glen had witnessed the assault and became more thoroughly enraged than anyone knew it was possible for him to get. Glen didn't get mad often — rarely, in fact — but this time he was furious.

As Bobby told it: "He grabbed another player friend and both went into the game. They made it their sole mission to take the player who had assaulted me out of the game. They didn't bother to play the play they were supposed to. They went in to take him out, and that's exactly what they did. One went high and one went low, and they took him down. They took him out. Our team suffered a 15-yard penalty for it.

"When Glen and the other guy came back, Glen looked at me and said, 'Well, Bobby, we got him for you!'"

"I thought that was just about one of the nicest things anyone ever did for me in my life — I still do," Bobby said.

Later on, Glen was the only one who stood up for Bobby when he quit the team in a fit of anger. Bobby was stretched thin already. He needed to work to make money and he worked on the farm. Football ate into his schedule even more.

But the straw that broke the camel's back came one day during practice when they were sophomores. It was incredibly hot and they had been practicing for hours. That part of Northwest Florida has the type of humidity that can push the actual temperature up 10 degrees.

"The coach ran us, ran us, and ran us, and he called all the seniors and juniors and said they could go get some water. But he told us to do more laps," Bobby said. "Well I was thirsty, so I decided to go get some water anyway. I asked the coach, 'Are we a team?' The coach said, 'Yes.' So I said, 'Well, then I am going to get water, too.'"

That's when that coach started screaming, yelling, and cursing at Bobby.

Bobby repeated himself. "I told him that if the seniors were getting water, I was going to get water, too. The coach kept yelling at me, so I grabbed my helmet, yanked it off my head and threw it just as far as I could throw, and I threw up my arms and I quit the team right there and then," Bobby said.

Glen, who had watched all this, began quietly shaking his head.

But later on, he went up to Bobby and said, "Bobby, you did well. If you're going to quit the team, that's the way to quit the team."

"Glen was the only one on the team that stood up for me," Bobby said. "The other guys lost respect for me, but Glen didn't. I don't think it would have occurred to him to stop being my friend. He was just that way."

CHAPTER SEVEN

PLAIN VANILLA AND ROCKY ROAD

Glen and his friend Bobby Hudson were alike in certain ways, but completely opposite in others. Glen was solid, calm, even-tempered and reliable, like plain vanilla ice cream. Bobby was more Rocky Road, lots of emotion and impulsive energy.

Glen and Bobby drove like maniacs wherever they went. "Glen had a dune buggy and an old, old jeep that you used to have to crank to start it up. That jeep would beat you to death whenever you rode in it. And Glen had the green Ford Mustang, so conspicuous that it was known all over town. That car wasn't an understated medium-green; it was very nearly the color of one of those glow-in-the-dark tree frogs."

They were in Glen's Mustang driving down a dirt road one afternoon. "The Dukes of Hazard" was a popular TV program about that time. The pair of teenagers decided to duplicate the hot-rodding antics that the rowdy characters performed in the show. First, they decided it would be fun to drive full throttle at about eighty miles an hour on that rough road. Then they got it into their heads to just go ahead and spin that Mustang round and round in circles. At first, they spun the car in circles. But then the car began spinning them in circles. It went out of control. They hadn't been counting on that. It scared them. When they finally stopped, they were so shaken they mutually agreed never to do that again.

During that year, the school let out for one of those snow days you almost never get in Northwest Florida . "Now if you let a Southern boy with all that pent-up energy out of school on a snow day, you are just asking for trouble," Bobby said.

The boys in the class decided to have a snowball fight. But they didn't throw ordinary snowballs. They decided to make "special" snowballs. Back then, all the boys either chewed tobacco or dipped snuff. They hollowed out the snowballs and spit big gooey wads of tobacco into the hole, then threw them as far as they could.

That might have been a fair fight until Glen became the one throwing the snowballs. People were familiar with the power of Glen's throwing arm. When people saw those things flying, they ran in all directions to get out of the way.

Glen and his friend were curious, impetuous teenagers who liked to try new things, whether or not they knew what they were doing. Glen was generally up for most things. It was never "Should we do this?" but rather "Why not do this?" There was never a question. It never crossed their minds to not do a thing.. With the brash confidence of teenagers, they thought they could do anything or figure out how if they didn't already know. Often enough, they did.

One time, Glen agreed to help Bobby remodel his car. Bobby had been drinking a good bit of tequila, and he persuaded Glen to help him swap out his bucket seats for a bench seat so that he and his girlfriend could sit closer together.

Glen wasn't much of a drinker. He might drink a beer occasionally, but mostly he was too busy laughing at the antics of all the people around him who were drinking.

Neither one of them had any idea what they were doing, but that almost never mattered to them. Usually, they decided they wanted to do something, and then they'd figure out how, by trial and error. If something didn't fit, they just wedged and wiggled it around until it did fit. If something sounded like a good idea, they went for it — the blind leading the blind — and figured out how to get it done.

The two swapped out the seats.

But when Glen suggested that they drill additional holes for two more bolts to secure the seat, Bobby said there wasn't enough time and anyway, it probably wasn't necessary. He regretted that. Later, as he was driving his newly remodeled automobile down the road, that bench seat flipped all the way backward like a recliner into the back seat.

Bobby called Glen back and told him he was right about the bolts. Glen usually was right about such things. He had an innate gift for construction and mechanical things. All his life Glen thrived on the challenge of figuring out some new project.

Glen was Glen wherever he was — in the house, out of the house, in public, in private and behind closed doors. Glen accepted people the way they were, without judgment. He may have rolled his eyes a time or two, but his loyalty was never in question.

"Glen was the only person I could ever really talk to," Bobby said. "We understood each other. We almost could tell what the other one was thinking before he said anything. He was the one person in the world that I knew — without a doubt — that I could trust. If I told him something in confidence, it went into his brain and it stayed there forever. He never once betrayed anyone's confidence.

"We never ever said one cross word to one another. There might be gaps of time when we didn't see each other, sometimes very long gaps. But it never changed anything between us. It could go a year, even. Then I would call him or he would call me, and we picked right back up where we always were," Bobby said. "He was more of a brother to me than the brothers I have."

My friend Mona Lusk is like that for me.

RONNIE AND GLEN ON ONE OF THEIR ADVENTURES!

CHAPTER EIGHT

SMALL TOWN DATING

After Bobby approved of Glen, we started dating, or whatever passes for dating when you're fourteen years old. We became a couple right then and we never looked back.

We weren't of driving age, so Glen would peddle his bicycle all the way over to my house and peddle back home later. It's not a great distance by car, but by bicycle over rough country roads, it's a more impressive 10-plus miles. I remember thinking that he must really like me a lot to do that.

After we met, we were together, or on the phone with each other all the time. It could be a point of contention at the Maholovich house because that was long before the days of call waiting or answering machines. In our early days, our dates consisted of Friday night ball games — baseball or football, depending on the season. He played and I watched him play. I would wait for him after a game and he would take me home.

Glen was a phenomenal athlete, naturally gifted. It was a toss-up whether he liked baseball or football better. He loved them both.

Eventually, after we were old enough to drive, we spent every bit of our dating time in somebody's car. At that time, Friday night dating activities for all teenagers in our town consisted of piling as many people as would fit into one car and driving back and forth between the only two small local eateries in the town.

The Ponderosa and the McMurphy's Dairy Bar were small mom-and-pop quick food places. McMurphy's was a drive-in with carhops. All the kids hung out between those two places. Our dating was small-town, country-style dating. The kind of dating people do if there isn't much in the way of local entertainment. There weren't skating rinks or bowling alleys. Malls existed but not anywhere around us. So we just hung out. It's not all that different from young people "hanging out" now.

First, we would park our cars, and then stuff as many people as we could fit into one person's car and head out. The perimeters of our territory were the roads between and surrounding the Ponderosa and McMurphy's Dairy Bar. So we drove from the Ponderosa restaurant to "downtown," which is what we called Atmore. Then we'd all go to the Dairy Bar. They had the best hamburgers. Sometimes we added corners to the loop and swung past the tennis court, then back to the Dairy Bar.

On our dates, we listened to eight-track music tapes and talked on CB radios, which were popular at the time. Back then, eight tracks were cutting edge technology. We listened to Creedence Clearwater Revival, Lynyrd Skynyrd, Bad Company, Alice Cooper. (Well, Glen liked Alice Cooper, but I didn't really.) We listened to Carol King. Electric Light Orchestra. Lots of Southern Rock and Roll. Glen especially loved Phil Collins and used to turn the radio up whenever one of his songs came on.

Glen found humor wherever he could. He couldn't help but laugh at slapstick, even if it wasn't supposed to be funny. Glen loved to laugh and he could find humor in practically any situation.

There was a time when Bobby was out with a date. It was really raining, but Bobby had stopped the car to repair the malfunctioning horn or malfunctioning turn signal, whichever one was causing the car's horn to blow whenever he flipped on the turn signal.

When Glen and I saw them, we pulled up.

At the time, Bobby was leaning in under the hood. Suddenly his date turned on the blinker. The horn blasted right into Bobby's ear, causing him to jump up and hit the hood of the car with tremendous force. It just about knocked Bobby out. And even though that sort of thing isn't supposed to be funny, it sent Glen into gales of laughter. He rolled his eyes and laughed his head off. He couldn't seem to help it.

Sometimes we went parking, which meant one couple—or two if we were on a double date — in one car, parked in a secluded area in order to express our affection privately. Except that, it wasn't always all that private. There was one particular place where we all parked, and all the cars were lined up in rows. We recognized one another's cars, so we would look around to see who else was there.

Glen's fondness for speeding got the better of him during one date. One particular night, we were riding around as always, and came to a red traffic light. We were waiting for the light to turn green when a friend pulled up beside us. The two guys in the other car looked over at us and started revving their motors, challenging us to an impromptu drag race.

Glen accepted the challenge and as soon as the light turned green, both drivers floored their accelerators and raced full out.

Naturally, a law enforcement officer spotted us. To our dismay, we heard that siren and saw blue lights flashing. We stopped, chagrined. Both drivers received tickets and our evening out on the town ended. Glen headed home to his parents with ticket in hand.

All in all, our courtship was typical of the times and the place where we lived.

PART TWO
GROWN-UPS

ANSLEIGH'S DANCE RECITAL

CHAPTER NINE

MARRIAGE AND CHILDREN

In due course, we graduated, and soon after, we got married. That may be unusual today, but back then, where we lived, it was common. Our high school had about ten sweetheart couples and all but two of them are still together. I went on to nursing school. Even though Glen could have attended college on a football scholarship, he was weary of academics and impatient to begin grownup life. He bypassed college and went straight to work.

There was only one person we knew that Glen would deliberately avoid if he could. It was hard to get on Glen's wrong side. Glen was so completely accepting of people, he rarely met a person he didn't like. But my mother, Doris, had a way of getting on his nerves. He was cordial to her, of course. But my mother was like fingernails on a chalkboard for him. We were all amused by their polite-but-prickly relationship.

She was outspoken, opinionated, and the sort of free-spirited person who would have been at Woodstock if she could have. She would love to have given birth to me in the back of a Volkswagen bus, painted all over with daisies and peace signs, with puffy letters spelling out "peace." If she could have gotten away with it, she would have preferred to name me Moonbeam or Starshine or Psychedelia. Some crazy thing like that

Nearly everyone who describes Glen talks about his strength, his levelheadedness, and his leadership qualities. He was not easily rattled. He was the person people relied on to remain calm under pressure.

That all evaporated the morning I went into labor with our first child. I awakened that morning with a backache that would not go away. However, pregnancy comes with so many aches, pains, inconveniences and discomforts that I dismissed it. I had a doctor appointment that day, anyway, so I went ahead to the appointment.

The doctor determined that my backache was early labor and directed me to go ahead to the hospital to check in. That's when Glen lost it. He was so nervous and excited that he got utterly lost driving to the hospital. While that might be understandable almost any place else in the world, in our little town the hospital was two blocks — blocks, not miles — from my doctor's office. To this day, we cannot imagine what convoluted mental GPS Glen used to throw him so far off course.

All went fine after we finally arrived, though. Our beautiful little daughter, Marcy, was born. Glen and I wanted our children to be closer in age than we had been with our siblings. We both had siblings separated in age by at least seven years. Because of that, we have such different memories of growing up together. A fourteen-year-old has little in common with a seven-year-old.

Jacob was born twenty-six months later, by which time Glen had learned the way to the hospital. Our children's personalities and interests are different, but they are loving and close to one another. Our daughter is ambitious and goal-oriented. Jacob is more laid-back. We were proud of the people they grew up to be.

We took our parental roles seriously. As time went on, Glen regretted his decision to bypass college, so he made it his mission to convince the children to avoid his mistake. Our daughter didn't need convincing, but our son Jacob had the same casual take-it-or-leave-it attitude toward college that Glen did at that age. Glen was able to convince Jacob to get his college degree, but sadly, did not live long enough to see him graduate.

Glen was determined that his children be fully prepared for adulthood. He believed it was his duty to provide them with a solid spiritual foundation and to send them into the world as happy, responsible, self-reliant people. To that end, he needed to teach them to be able to do for themselves as much as they possibly could.

Being country people meant that we grew up doing many things for ourselves that city people often pay others to do. Glen tried to pass along whatever knowledge or expertise that he had to his children, whether it be navigating a river, planting a flowerbed or hanging a door. And he succeeded. He was still trying desperately to do these things with his grandchildren long after he was too ill to do so. The grandchildren were his life. He adored them and they adored him right back.

Zachary, who goes by Zac, was born when Jacob was just seventeen years old. The announcement of Zac's pending birth came as quite a shock to us. We knew that fatherhood, as a teenager, could be an obstacle to the bright future we had envisioned for Jacob. We turned out to be wrong.

And, as for our grandson, about a month after Zachary was born, my daughter and I both looked at each other and said, "How did we ever get by without this wonderful child?"

It turned out that Zac is the only grandchild to have any memory of Glen before his illness. Zac remembers the strong, healthy Glen who took him fishing and boating. Now he is able to share those memories with his sister, Ansleigh. Glen had already been diagnosed by the time Ansleigh was two years old. She often asks her brother to tell her stories about Glen in his healthy days.

"I've seen pictures," Ansleigh said. "But I don't remember him then."

Today Ansleigh is a pretty, tow-haired girl with bright eyes that seem to be always watching, observing and assessing her surroundings. Thoughtful and circumspect, she is the studious reader in the family and more mature than her years would suggest.

She does have wonderful memories of her grandfather, just none of them when he was healthy. "He used to take me to my ballet lessons," Ansleigh said. "He was always the only man in a room full of ladies." Glen didn't mind that a bit.

Even later, when Glen could no longer speak or move anything except the lower part of his body, he was a fully participating grandfather. He entertained the children, all of us, with his puppet shows.

"He would have socks on his feet and make them be puppets," Ansleigh said. The children performed the speaking parts. He manipulated his sock-covered feet across the top of a coffee table "stage" to perform the puppet action. The whole family loved those puppet shows.

Ansleigh wishes her time with her grandfather could have been longer, but said she doesn't feel one bit cheated. In fact, she believes her experiences with her grandfather enriched her life.

"I think I got something extra. I think seeing him when he was sick and being able to help him, gave me something extra that other kids don't have," Ansleigh said. "I think I understand things about sick people that other kids don't. I am not glad that he was sick, but I am glad that I got to be around him."

CHAPTER TEN

DAY JOB

G len worked as a collections officer at the First National Bank and Trust of Atmore, the person people dealt with when they defaulted on loan payments. He detested the part of his job that required him to actually repossess property. Glen agonized over those things. He much preferred to help people figure out some way that they could repay their loan and still keep their things.

Unfortunately, he was not always successful.

He disliked taking away people's property so much that he was taking classes to become a loan officer, so that he could put that part of his job behind him. He was close to finishing when he was diagnosed with ALS.

When Glen did have to take possession of someone's property, he did so with such compassion that most people understood that he did not want to; that it was his job and he had no choice. Even they held him in high regard.

Our dear friend Gerald McAnally, who worked with Glen part-time, saw Glen's emotional turmoil regularly. At that time, Gerald was working for Frito-Lay during the day, and worked with Glen to make extra money.

We first met Gerald at the church we all attended around 1995 and became close friends. After that, Gerald became Glen's roommate whenever they went on one of their church mission trips.

Gerald remembers when Glen had to collect furniture from a family after they defaulted on their payments. Glen was upset at the parents for not taking better care of their family.

"I think it grieved him more than anything to take the furniture away from the children. I think he ended up leaving the mattresses for the children," Gerald said.

Gerald thinks that such encounters might have been part of the reason behind Glen's extreme frugality. That's possible, but I doubt it, because Glen had that trait long before he worked at the bank.

Glen had limits to his patient understanding, though. He didn't get outwardly angry often—most people have trouble remembering any time that he did—but parental negligence and irresponsibility just about sent him over the edge.

Sometimes, when he went to a family's house to discuss their situation with the bank, the children answered the door and told him their parents were not home, even though Glen knew they were. He also knew the idea for the children to lie did not originate with them.

Obviously, the parents had told them to lie. That incensed Glen. He could not understand how any parent could purposely teach a child to be dishonest. That was so contrary to everything that Glen believed about parenting, he could barely stand it.

He did not rant or even confront the parents. But if you knew him, and you were around him, you could sense how angry and disappointed he was. He hurt for the children.

Although most people whose property Glen repossessed completely understood that Glen was not responsible for their plight, a few did not. Some people became quite angry. They saw Glen taking their property, so they blamed him for the problem.

Like most people, Glen left his work at work. He didn't talk to me about the particulars of his job. But every so often, he would make a point of asking me where I intended to work that day in my capacity as a home health nurse.

Then, after I told him, he would caution me. "You might want to go somewhere else today." That's when I knew that someone living in that area was mad at Glen, although I didn't know who it was.

Every so often, it was quite a bit more obvious. People pointedly snubbed us.

One day, a lady snubbed us in church. It was completely unexpected and I was astonished. I was especially shocked because it happened at church. I whispered to Glen, "What is her problem, why is she acting like that?"

He looked at me and said, "It isn't about us. It isn't about you. It's about something with the bank."

"Oh."

Glen did not take other people's slights personally. He understood that people's anger was about the situation, and not about him, even when they themselves didn't know that.

Sometimes he suggested I avoid certain areas. Other times we could not even go inside a particular restaurant to eat. That sort of thing didn't happen often, but it did happen. If we wanted food from that restaurant, we had to order it under a different name and then pick it up at the drive-through window. It is a small town, and like all small towns, everyone generally knows everyone else. The name Maholovich is a rare name as it is, but in our town, Maholovich meant us.

CHAPTER ELEVEN

LANDSCAPING

G len worked in the office at the bank during the day, but during the early morning hours, he maintained the bank's landscaping. He took care of the grounds, the plants and the flowers, everything. And he did that job as he did every other job, perfectly and professionally.

He insisted on perfection, to the point of driving anyone working with him completely nuts. Gerald, who worked with him on landscaping too, remembers his extreme perfectionism. He recalls that Glen insisted that plants be measured out precisely, planted at exactly equal depths and exactly equal distances apart. He was insistent. Gerald took it all in stride.

But the one person especially exasperated by Glen's perfectionism was our son. Jacob worked with his father at the bank pulling weeds and helping with the landscaping, even when he was young.

Today Jacob is like his father, tall, handsome and naturally athletic. He is articulate, polite, and very Southern Alabama. He was in ROTC in school and served with the National Guard in Iraq. He, too, is highly skilled at woodworking and he loves outdoors activities.

Glen was not a "Cat's-in-the-Cradle" type of father — the Harry Chapin song about a father who promises to be with his son, but is too busy for one reason or another to ever do so. He was very hands-on.

"He made me do it perfectly. I hated that. I thought he was being mean," Jacob said. "Now I understand that my work reflected on him with the people at the bank, which meant that my work had to be of as high quality as his was."

He speaks highly of his father now. But during the years when Jacob worked with his father, he was also beginning to assert his individuality and trying on some independence. There were some father-son rough patches.

"You know when you're fifteen, you think you know it all, and your parents don't know anything," Jacob said. "I went to school, I had a regular job, and I didn't want to go to the bank and pull weeds, too. I was tired. I was a teenager. I just did not want to pull weeds."

His father's widely known reputation for excellence put even more pressure on Jacob, even when he wasn't working with his father. "People would find out who I was, and they'd say, 'Oh, you're Glen Maholovich's son.' Automatically people expected my work to be a higher standard, too," Jacob said.

Jacob's son, Zac, is now about the same age that Jacob was when he worked for Glen. That offers Jacob an entirely different perspective of his own growing up.

"It wasn't until I became a father myself that I began to see things from his point of view and to appreciate what he gave us. He taught us responsibility and self-reliance and to work for what we wanted. I think lots of parents don't do that so much anymore. I realize now that I was one of the lucky ones to have the parents I had."

Everyone who knew Glen knew that his family came first, before everything else. He'd drop everything on a workday to travel miles away to our daughter's university to come to her aid. Marcy doesn't remember the specifics of the catastrophes that brought him to her, but said that's exactly the kind of thing he did.

She is intelligent, purpose-driven and forthright. She took Glen's work ethic to heart. She has always been ambitious, and that is reflected in her professional success. "We always worked for whatever we wanted. If we wanted to take a vacation, we went and worked on somebody's house," she said.

Glen often repeated an ancient Chinese proverb. If he said it once, he said it a thousand times, "Give a man a fish, and feed him for a day. Teach a man to fish, feed him for a lifetime." Later, Glen questioned whether he had done all he should for his children, but the fact is that he was extraordinarily successful at teaching our children "how to fish."

CHAPTER TWELVE

GLEN'S TRUE PASSION: WOODWORKING

Everyone in our family has a strong work ethic, but no one worked longer or harder than Glen did. The banking and the landscaping were things he did, but his real passion was building, remodeling, renovating and doing all manner of woodworking.

He had an artisan's hands. He could make something out of nothing and it would be beautiful. He wasn't quite as good at the artistic-creative side of things, but I have always had an eye for that. I developed designs and he made them happen. Our whole family has always been a naturally good team, which became a critical factor in our ability to cope later when Glen became ill. We seemed to know what to do, when to do it and which of us should do it, without a lot of discussion.

Glen did not just build an occasional bookshelf or entertainment center. He built furniture. He renovated rooms or houses. He built anything and everything. If a thing could be built or fabricated by his hand — and most things could — he said, "I can do this myself, so I am going to do it. Why should I pay someone else to do it?"

He had an innate gift. He began working, designing, and creating handmade furniture pieces back in his teen years. He always had a project or two or three going at the same time. He rolled from project to project, scarcely coming up for air. It wasn't unusual for Glen to come home in the evenings and turn right back around to leave to work on some project. I felt like our lives were all about finishing projects.

For a couple of years, Glen spent every single weekend helping to build an addition to our church. We had strong words about that. "EVERY weekend?" I asked him. "Why does it have to be every single weekend?"

Sometimes, Glen could be a little obsessive.

Gerald recalled, "I'll never forget the bedroom furniture he built for his daughter's apartment when she went away to college. That was around '98 or '99. That furniture was just beautiful and as professional and nice, or nicer, than anything you would buy at a store. It was of the highest quality," Gerald said. "I know, because I helped deliver it and it weighed about four tons."

Glen's frugality was at least part of the reason Glen built that furniture. Glen was always saving, Gerald said. "He got his money's worth on that lawnmower he used to cut grass at the bank. That thing was about to fall apart, and he would still use it. It was as if having to spend a dollar would just about kill him. He was frugal across the board.

"We had a relationship more like brothers. I don't remember ever having a cross word with him." But like brothers, they disagreed sometimes. One such time was over the setting of a thermostat.

"During a hurricane, we stayed with them," Gerald said. One of Glen's habits was to keep the thermostat set high in the summer.

"It got hot. So every time I'd go to the bathroom, I'd put it down."

Glen fussed. "Who's putting that air down?" And Glen would push the thermostat back up high again. Then Gerald got hot again, so he pushed the thermostat back down.

A little bit later, Glen would push it back up.

And a little later, Gerald pushed it back down again.

This went on. And on. It got to be a running battle between them.

Gerald remembers that it was always vitally important to Glen that he provide for his family. "He was passionate about that," Gerald said. His concern for the welfare of his family plagued him grievously when he was ill.

CHAPTER THIRTEEN

GLEN'S VOICE

Long before we knew the reason, the symptom of ALS that people noticed first about Glen was the dramatic change in the sound of his voice. Its tenor changed and his words were sometimes slurred and raspy.

It turns out this is the most common early symptom of Bulbar Onset ALS. Speech becomes increasingly difficult as the patient loses the ability to control his tongue properly — dysarthria. The tongue may become noticeably smaller and start to twitch. As the condition progresses, speech problems become significantly worse and the patient has difficulties swallowing — dysphagia.

Glen used to say that it felt like he always had something stuck in his throat.

The tongue is primarily responsible for producing the sounds that become words. In Bulbar Onset ALS, the tongue eventually becomes ineffective. Additionally, the energy for speech and sound comes from breath support. When a person breathes in and prepares to speak, the vocal cords come together. Pressure builds up below them. When the person starts speaking, the vocal cords move apart, allowing that air to rush between them, causing them to vibrate quickly. The vibration is what generates the sound. Without adequate breath support, such as with an ALS patient, the patient is unable to produce much volume or speak long sentences.

Beside those impediments, the soft palate no longer elevates as before. When that happens, the sound that is produced goes up into and out through the nasal cavity. It is like that sound made by speaking through pinched nostrils — hypernasality — and has a profound effect on the sound of speech.

Glen's strange-sounding voice was the first thing Whitney McGill noticed when she came home from college. The McGill family was lifelong friends of ours. In the final years of Glen's illness, Whitney became deeply involved in helping us. Our two families attended the same church, and Whitney's father and Glen had played baseball together as children. Whitney and Jacob were married the year after Glen passed away.

When Whitney first heard Glen's voice after she came home, she was shocked.

"Before, Glen had such a deep loud voice," Whitney said. "Then it changed drastically."

Whitney had long admired Glen. For one thing, Glen reminded her of her own father, "He was a tightwad, too," Whitney laughed. She said she knew that she could go to Glen with anything if her father was not around.

Whitney is a pretty, petite, and soft-spoken young woman whose appearance might suggest that she is a children's librarian or a bank teller. She is a cop, a parole officer. Her degree is in Criminal Justice. At work, she must be firm and authoritative. But when Whitney talks about Glen, she tears up, then laughs at the incongruity. "I know tears don't exactly fit in with what I do for a job." But she separates her professional life from her personal life.

Glen held an honored place in her heart for other reasons, as well. "When I was in high school, my parents separated for a while, and Glen stood by my Daddy. Of course, Vanessa was there for my Mom." In the end, though, she said that Glen was helpful with her parents' decision to reconcile. Many others were drawn to Glen as well.

As a member of the church's prayer team, Glen was one of the people who would pray for other people who requested special prayers. He continued to do that even when he was so ill he had trouble walking and no one could understand a single word he spoke. He continued to do it because people continued to ask him.

Whitney said she always wanted Glen to be the one to pray for her.

"When our family was going through some things, I wanted Glen to pray for me because it was personal and he knew the situation.

Later, after he was diagnosed, I still wanted him to be the one to pray for me because I felt like he was closer to God that any other person there. And I know I wasn't the only person who felt that way. Just hearing his voice, even when you couldn't understand him, and knowing how hard it was for him to do what he was doing was so inspiring and uplifting for me. He would pray, get winded and you couldn't understand his words, but it didn't matter to anyone. It was profoundly moving."

Glen continued doing it as long as he possibly could. Finally, when he lost the use of his hands so that he could no longer hold the bottle of anointing oil that was part of the ritual, Glen stepped down from the prayer team.

CHAPTER FOURTEEN

GLEN'S VALUES

Many people only begin praying when adversity strikes, but I have prayed all my life. I pray to God exactly the same way that I talk to a friend. It's a very natural part of my daily life. It was not that way with Glen. Glen didn't grow up going to church and knew little about faith, spirituality or religion.

He only started coming to church regularly after we started dating, more for me than for a genuine religious feeling, I think. I realized how little he knew when he did not know who significant characters in the Bible were. But then Glen began to learn more and his personal faith increased. As time went on, Glen's faith grew independent of my influence, and he came to rely upon it.

That he was late in coming to his faith was a source of some regret for Glen. But most people who knew him would say that he more than made up for that by the qualities of compassion, service and spirituality he demonstrated in his everyday life.

His faith was never a thing he used to impress others, nor a thing that he felt he needed to hide. He inspired people, not by proselytizing, but by the way he treated people and the way he lived.

"He was better than I was," Bobby said. "He showed compassion. Just knowing Glen, just being around him, made you look at yourself and re-evaluate your own actions and made you want to be a better person. There was just something about him that made you want to be accountable."

Glen would defend other people, but he let slights toward him roll off his own back. Someone would do something bad to him, or rude or ugly, and even though other people would want to go do something about it, Glen would say, "No . . . I'm not going to do anything."

Glen was always Glen, wherever he was. There was no "public Glen" and a different "private Glen." It's about impossible to find anyone who can remember him ever saying a bad word about anyone. And he didn't complain. That just wasn't him. He was relentlessly optimistic.

"I think the worst thing I ever heard him say about anything, was one time. He said, 'It sucks.' That's all. Just that. Just once," Bobby said.

Glen's illness was the first thing that ever caused his boyhood friend to ask God, "Why?" It made so many people question why God would allow a good person like Glen to acquire this horrible illness. At the same time, Glen's grace, humor, and fearlessness during his illness inspired those same people.

Glen himself wondered why God would allow this particular disease, one that would rob him of his gift to provide service to others. But he did accept it. He used to say, "No one knows the whole picture."

"Glen showed me a different level of faith," Bobby said. "He never complained; he never got bitter. He truly made me re-examine my relationship with God."

Glen had the ability to take people exactly as they were. He was interested in really knowing people on a deep level. He almost never wanted to talk about himself. He wanted to talk about you. He wanted to know who you were. He wanted to understand people and really get to know them as human beings. He was not judgmental. He never suggested that anyone be anything but who they were. He never gave advice.

He demonstrated how to live, always on the high road, by example, by how he lived. He might talk about his faith to very close friends, but as a rule he didn't bring it up unless you asked him directly. He was an incredibly humble, unassuming man.

Everyone agrees that he was a role model for many people, but we never dared to say so to him. The idea that anyone would consider him a role model would have struck him as very funny.

CHAPTER FIFTEEN

MISSION TRIPS

Before Glen got sick, he was hard to slow down. He was an unstoppable force of nature. Glen worked at the bank, he landscaped, he built and remodeled things, and he went on church missions to South America, scarcely stopping for breath.

Glen carried his faith, his woodworking skills, his enthusiasm and his sense of humor on mission trips to South America five different times, where he helped build churches and orphanages.

Glen loved building. He loved helping people. Putting those together put two of his favorite things into the same package.

Gerald was with Glen in 2003, when he took his fifth and final church mission trip to South America; a time when he was starting to exhibit symptoms of his then-undiagnosed illness.

"I never saw any signs of his illness while we were working together," Gerald recalled.

Gerald remembers that last trip as one during which he fell victim to Glen's sense of humor. Gerald, it should be noted, is a gregarious man of considerable girth.

"We were staying in cottages in the Andes Mountains in Ecuador," Gerald said. "There were no screens on the windows; there was no air conditioning, either, so we kept the windows open."

They all knew that the hot water in the cottages lasted only so long, so Gerald always rushed to get the first shower. One particular time, he rushed in to get the first shower and threw all his clothes on the bed. He took his shower and then settled in for the evening.

"Later, when I got into bed and the lights were off, I felt something in my bed that shouldn't be there," Gerald said. "I knew the windows were open and I knew there were snakes around. Naturally, I put two and two together."

"I got scared. I jumped out of bed screaming, 'There's a snake in my bed! There's a snake in my bed!' I was scared to death."

Glen volunteered to check it out. He cautiously stepped over to Gerald's bed, where he looked for the snake. After about a minute, Glen called back to Gerald. But he was laughing.

"Oh, Gerald, I've got it," Glen said between chuckles. "And boy, is it ever a big one!"

Gerald hollered back. "What do you mean, you got it?"

Glen just kept laughing. "I said, I've got it," he repeated.

By this time, Gerald was frightened — but also very confused.

Finally, Glen showed Gerald the 'snake,' still laughing and trying to catch his breath. "It was my great big, long belt," Gerald said.

The truth was that throughout his illness, no matter how sick he was, Glen never lost his sense of humor. He loved laughing and he loved having people laugh with him. After Glen died, one of the men who went on a mission with him said that he could still hear Glen's laughter in his mind.

Gerald eulogized Glen at his funeral eight years later.

CHAPTER SIXTEEN

KEITH AND DEBBIE LISENBY

K eith Lisenby was one of Glen's close friends who had known Glen for a few years before his illness. The two of them had building in their blood. The difference is that Keith is a contractor and Glen did his woodworking on the side. But they spoke the same language of woodworking and craftsmanship.

"When we first met, Glen was like me," Keith said. "Glen was good with his hands and he could build anything."

We met Keith and Debbie Lisenby about 1998, when the couple attended the funeral for Debbie's grandfather at the church Glen and I attended. They were impressed by the preacher there. After that, they started attending, despite the long drive they had to make each week.

"We lived so far from the church, it required a forty to forty-five minute drive each way. We drove to church on Sunday morning, and then we drove all the way back home, and that night we drove back up again," Debbie said.

One day, Glen suggested that they not drive back home, but rather that they spend the afternoon with us at our house. This was before we really knew them very well.

Debbie and Keith accepted.

"They fed us lunch and even told us we could take naps if we wanted to. They were so gracious," Debbie said.

Naturally, we all became good friends.

Glen absolutely thrived on social interaction. He loved being with people. When he saw a person he knew, he didn't just wave. He went over to them. "I remember going into restaurants with Glen, and he would walk around to different tables and talk to people he knew," Keith said. "If he didn't talk to you, it was because he didn't see you."

Building and fabricating things with wood was the basis of Glen and Keith's friendship at first. But when Glen got sick and lost the use of his hands and arms, he could no longer do the things that the two had in common. "At that point, we began an entirely new, deeper type of relationship," Keith said.

Watching Glen, who had once been so physically active, suddenly lose those abilities, was painful for all of us. But seeing how Glen handled his infirmities inspired Keith, as it did so many others.

"He never, ever got bitter or angry. He would get tired. But he never, ever seemed like he was tempted to give up. He lived his life," Keith said.

As I have said before, Glen was not a perfect man. Even after Glen lost his own abilities, he didn't mind critiquing others' work.

Glen used to watch Keith work and then critique him. I was chagrined. He was an amateur critiquing a professional. Even if he was a talented amateur, he was critiquing a professional.

Keith was remarkably understanding. "I realized that I could be in his circumstances — that anyone could be — at any time. It was very difficult for Glen to let that all go. It's a man thing. It's a cultural man thing, particularly in the Deep South," Keith said.

CHAPTER SEVENTEEN

BUILDING HOPE

For a while, after he was already ill but before he knew what was the cause, Glen operated our non-profit organization to help repair the houses and build wheelchair ramps for disabled and elderly people who had no resources, finances or family to do it. We called it Building Hope. It operated about three years before the symptoms of Glen's illness became too great for him to continue.

Building Hope came about through a set of coincidental — or not-so-coincidental — circumstances.

One day I came home after visiting an elderly woman patient whose home was falling apart. She had no money for repairs, no relatives who could assist her and there were no agencies to help.

I knew that some simple repairs could enhance the quality of her life tremendously, but I could not figure out any way for her to get them done.

What I did not know was that at just about that same time, my friend Mona Lusk had been approached by two men in her Sunday school class. They were seeking ways to use their carpentry skills to help others. Mona told them she didn't know of anything right then, but she would keep her eyes open. Mona is an enthusiastic, pretty blonde with a wide-open heart, energy, and optimism to spare.

Mona knew nothing about my concerns for my elderly patient and I didn't know about the two carpenters looking for service opportunities. Then one day Mona and I had lunch and I told her about the lady with the crumbling house. She told me about the two men with carpentry skills. Light bulbs flashed and we put the carpenters to work on the patient's crumbling house.

After that, it occurred to us both that there might be people in similar situations. We began to wonder if we could establish a nonprofit organization that could help other needy people.

There are some wonderful organizations like that in other places. And in other places, the funds are provided by the Homeowners Association or the Builders Association, but we didn't have that in our rural, sparsely populated area.

But we didn't want to let it go. We became convinced that those previous coincidences weren't so coincidental after all. We strongly believed that this was something we were meant to do. As improbable as it seemed, we decided we would go ahead. We would form a non-profit to provide emergency construction services at no cost to needy elderly and disabled homeowners who could not obtain repairs through traditional means.

We had no earthly idea what we were doing, of course. We had no funding nor did we have any idea where to get funding. We didn't have any idea what legal requirements we would need to meet. We didn't know much at all about what we were attempting to do. All we had was a good idea, a strong conviction and a sense of purpose.

Like Dorothy following the Yellow Brick Road, we decided to put one foot in front of the other and see how far we could go. We went from one place to another to seek legal advice, financial assistance and other guidance.

We were not automatically greeted with enthusiasm, or even common courtesy. In fact, one man dismissed us with rude condescension.

He called us "you two little girls," and told us the exorbitant fee his services would cost. That would have been funny if it hadn't been so disappointing. We had no funds to pay his bill. We were seeking funds. He couldn't quite grasp that we wanted to form a charitable organization to help people and that we had come to him seeking advice and guidance for funding. We didn't get any of that from him.

We were so naïve.

But we still believed that we were supposed to do this, so we headed back out and took each step as it presented itself. We were not ready to give up.

Soon we were going all over the place, speaking to civic groups and chambers of commerce and any other group that would let us speak.

One faltering step after another eventually led us to people who were not rude or dismissive. They were courteous and even enthusiastic about our project. They were helpful and didn't charge us anything. We met an attorney with a disabled relative, who was immediately interested. He helped us with the legal work at no cost. Soon, we were able to acquire funding and materials. In the end, all the labor and materials we needed were donated by businesses and volunteers.

Naturally, Glen became heavily involved. Glen imposed the same high standards on Building Hope projects as he did everything else. We began busily building ramps and making repairs to houses. At first, we were working out of our kitchens and cars.

Then there came a sad time when Mona's marriage ended, which meant that she needed a new home.

She had limited funds, but she found a perfect two-story house that was in foreclosure. It happened to be held by the same bank where Glen worked. It occurred to Mona that the house could double as both a residence for her on the upper level and an office for Building Hope on the ground floor. It would be perfect, she thought.

Naturally, the bank wanted a lot more money for the house than Mona could afford, but she went ahead and made the offer for an amount she could afford. Of course, the bank said no. However, the bank also agreed to hold on to her offer as a backup, while seeking other buyers.

Periodically Glen would update Mona with the disappointing news that there were potential buyers who seemed interested. In the end, though, the bank never did sell the house for the price they wanted. They accepted Mona's offer.

That meant Mona had a house and Building Hope had an office. We were sure Building Hope would provide help for needy people for a very long time.

TWO OF THE GREATEST JOYS OF GLEN'S LIFE. HIS FIRST GRANDCHILD, ZAC AND FISHING!

CHAPTER EIGHTEEN

BRUCE AND SUSAN LOVETT

We met Bruce and Susan Lovett through Building Hope, when we went to the home of Bruce's father to install a ramp for his wheelchair. We hit it off with them right away and became good friends. We socialized and took trips together. Some years later when Glen was ill, Bruce took him on one of his very last trips, one that turned out to be more of an adventure than either one of them wanted.

Bruce, a handsome, burly man with a mane of white hair, spent his career in law enforcement. Bruce is another one who has trouble speaking of Glen without a catch in his voice. He met Glen at the very early stages of his Lou Gehrig's disease, and watched sorrowfully and helplessly following the diagnosis as his friend gradually became increasingly incapacitated.

"Glen was a very special person," Bruce said. "I spent many years in law enforcement and I put a very high premium on courage and valor. But I cannot ever remember meeting anyone with as much courage and valor as Glen had."

Bruce brushes aside his own award for courage. "Hero is a word used for a lot of people who aren't really heroes," Bruce said. "People get called heroes for doing what needs to be done, doing the job they're trained to do," he said. Bruce pointed out that Glen had been thrust involuntarily into his situation, without warning and with no preparation. Glen had years to contemplate what was happening to him and he knew exactly what the outcome would be. Yet he soldiered on without complaint.

"I don't know about anyone else, but Glen was my hero. This man was a genuine hero."

Over the course of three years, Glen's symptoms increased in frequency and intensity. The day came when Glen's fatigue, loss of dexterity and muscle weakness prevented him from direct participation in Building Hope projects, though he still organized and oversaw projects.

But soon his voice began to change so dramatically that he was hard to understand. Even his behind-the-scenes participation had to end.

Glen had built or personally overseen the building of wheelchair ramps for other people, not realizing that a day would come when he would need one for himself. When that time finally did come, our son Jacob said that he was unexpectedly approached by a man at his church. "He found out that Daddy needed a wheelchair ramp." He said, "Don't worry about it. It is being taken care of."

After Glen was too ill to participate and I became overwhelmed by his care, Building Hope was forced to shut down. Later, my friend Mona carried her altruistic talents to Los Angeles, where she continues to help others at The Dream Center. The center is an impressive volunteer-driven organization that provides an array of much-needed services. Among them are residential rehabilitation programs for teens and adults, a shelter for victims of human trafficking, transitional shelter for homeless families, mobile hunger relief and medical programs, a foster care intervention outreach, as well as adult basic education, job skills training, and life skills counseling to homeless families and individuals.

I visit her in California and she visits me in Alabama.

PART THREE

MEDICAL MERRY-GO-ROUND

CHAPTER NINETEEN

PEANUT BUTTER

There came a point when the symptoms could no longer be dismissed or explained away. Something very real was wrong with Glen. The symptoms were getting worse and happening more often. It was 2004 and still, after three years, we had no idea what was causing Glen's strange condition.

The worst of his symptoms was the choking. One pleasant Sunday evening, we were at home in the house on State Line Road where Glen had grown up. We were chatting and eating peanut butter and crackers. It was like any other night.

Glen began to choke. Glen did have a habit of eating too much too fast, for which I sometimes scolded him. When he choked this time, I thought it was nothing more than that. But his choking didn't stop. It continued, becoming more and more severe. It was so terrifying that I realized this was not like ordinary choking. This was serious. I threw myself into professional nurse mode.

I attempted the Heimlich maneuver, in which a person wraps her arms around the choking victim from behind, then squeezes and thrusts upward with her fist in order to dislodge the obstruction. It didn't work, so I tried again. It still didn't work. I tried it several times.

It never did any good. Glen was still choking. No matter what I did, I simply could not dislodge the peanut butter, which now was adhering to his windpipe like some kind of sticky, edible Super Glue. He began turning blue. He clutched his throat with his hands, starved for oxygen.

He headed toward the door to go outside into the open air in a desperate attempt to find and inhale some oxygen. I followed close at his side, dialing 911 at the same time.

The situation was dire.

Glen fell to his knees, struggling to produce a cough sufficient to dislodge the obstruction in his throat. He was terrified and I was terrified. Panic was setting in. The 911 operator answered. Finally, just as I was speaking with the dispatcher, Glen managed to produce sufficient force to expel the peanut butter.

The memory of that event is so seared into my brain that to this day I have a visceral reaction of dread when I hear anyone choking.

The peanut butter event was terrifying, but after it ended, we figured that was that. People choke. Although still quite shaken, we heaved a sigh of relief, thinking we had learned our lesson about the grossly underreported dangers of eating peanut butter and crackers. It was terrifying, but it was over.

Glen naturally repeated the peanut butter story with a comic spin. He turned the story on its head, making it so funny that no one could help but laugh. The Sunday morning he told the story at our church, he left the congregation in gales of laughter. It bothered Glen for anyone to be uncomfortable around him. Humor became his tool to reassure others. With his worsening symptoms, he felt called upon to use humor more and more.

A long time after the fact, we learned this had not been ordinary choking. The end of Glen's choking episode had not come about because he managed to expel the peanut butter. There was a reason my attempts at the Heimlich maneuver failed to help.

This choking episode was not caused by bits of food having gone into his windpipe instead of his esophagus. His throat had experienced a spasm, similar to a foot cramp. That prevented him from inhaling oxygen and caused the choking. The patient is not actually choking because a tiny bit of air does find its way into the lungs. Later, after Glen was finally diagnosed, we learned that this type of choking is common with ALS patients. It is called "laryngospasm," and it occurs when a bit of saliva goes awry and causes the larynx, the vocal cords, to spasm. That closes off the airway. Just as a foot-cramp passes on its own, so does the throat spasm.

The life-saving Heimlich maneuver, which works so well for standard choking events, was of no use whatsoever in stopping Glen's throat spasms.

Glenn's choking episodes became so routine that mealtimes went from relaxing family events to high-tension drama. I became a hyper-vigilant soldier, on high alert for his inevitable choking.

When Glen choked, no one could help him.

It happened so often that, like how a new mother learns to recognize which of her baby's cries means that he hungry and which one means that he needs a nap, I learned to tell by the sound he made what stage of the spasm he was experiencing.

We never had peanut butter in our house again. Later we began to ban other types of foods. Certain foods were more likely to trigger a spasm. Soft foods were okay, watery foods were not. Glen's illness caused him to produce excessive saliva, which he could not control on his own. That often triggered a choking event. Later, after he knew what was wrong, he would choke on certain things that he liked, but he still insisted on eating them. As the disease progressed, he was apt to choke at any time, whether he was eating or not.

To sit by and watch helplessly is a wretched experience. To do so again and again is emotionally soul shattering. To do so in public is all that — with an audience.

Glen loved to go out to restaurants and I did not intend to stop him. However, if you didn't know what was going on, Glen's choking was a horrific sound. It sounded as if someone had placed a plastic bag over his head. It sounded as if someone were dying in front of you.

Once at a restaurant his choking spell clearly panicked the other diners. After he could breathe again, he looked around the restaurant and in his best stage voice, announced. "You might not want to eat the chicken." The diners laughed and resumed their meals.

He loved to eat and he enjoyed good food. But even more than food, he loved being with people. A few years later, when he could no longer eat by mouth, he still accompanied us to restaurants. He didn't care about the food. He cared about the company.

I secretly feared there would come a time when he might choke to death at any moment. I think the rest of the family did as well. It came to a point that the choking didn't seem to faze Glen nearly as much as it did those of us around him.

KEATON AND ELLA LOVING ON THEIR "BO"

CHAPTER TWENTY

WORSENING SYMPTOMS

By now, the symptoms had become frightening. There was no longer any way to dismiss them as not serious. Glen had begun choking on a regular basis. He grew fatigued easily and his muscles seemed to grow weaker by the day.

His once strong, deep voice had changed into something raspy and he was having trouble speaking. His muscles twitched and cramped. He had fevers. His tongue had begun quivering uncontrollably. We could think of no ailment these symptoms matched.

Glen had already been riding a medical merry-go-round for some time. He wearily dragged himself from one specialist to another, was poked, prodded, and examined in one medical test after another, each time receiving an entirely different theory as to what might be wrong, yet his symptoms remained a mystery.

ALS is perverse. It is a "Lucy-pulling-back-the-football-just-as-Charlie-Brown-runs-to-kick-it" disease that seems to wait until a patient and his family are comfortably settled before it pounces down hard to wreak chaos. Because ALS is uncommon, no one expects it. It usually arrives at precisely the point when lifelong dreams are coming to fruition. Worst of all, it enters out of left field, usually striking people who have no family history of the disease.

In that respect we were a textbook example. It happened at that time in our lives when the hard work and struggle of building a home and family had begun to ease and become comfortably routine. The kids were no longer kids, but adults off living their own lives. We were still relatively young, energetic and enthusiastic, with established careers. We were happily anticipating the next phase of our lives. And then our lives hit that wall of granite.

CHAPTER TWENTY-ONE

CHRISTMAS 2004 DIAGNOSIS

For a long time, none of Glen's doctors considered ALS. Because it is so rare and because his form of ALS is even more rare, it was not the first thing, or the second thing, or even the third thing that doctors looked into. There's a medical axiom that goes, "When you hear hoof beats, think horses, not zebras." That makes sense most of the time.

Finally, on December 21, 2004, Glen saw a neurosurgeon who seized upon a red flag that Glen's previous doctors had overlooked. We were thrilled. At long last, almost three years after Glen began experiencing symptoms, a doctor had some inkling of what might be wrong.

Then the doctor told us that Glen needed to see a neurologist specialist to have an EMG. Not next week. Not sometime after Christmas. But right away.

An electromyography (EMG) is a technique for evaluating and recording the electrical activity produced by skeletal muscles. An electromyograph detects the electrical potential generated by muscle cells when the cells are electrically activated. The signals can be analyzed to detect medical abnormalities.

We were startled by the doctor's sense of urgency. He wasted no time arranging a test. While still in his office he got on the phone and arranged for Glen to have the test performed by a specialist the following morning, December 22, 2004.

That sense of immediacy sent a cold, foreboding shiver throughout my body — the doctor suspected something much worse than anything we had imagined. The next morning we visited the specialist neurologist for the EMG.

I was not allowed to go in with Glen to the room where he was tested. He told me about it and later he wrote about it.

After exhaustive testing, the doctor reported that Glen had Lou Gehrig's disease.

My own memory of that office visit is a hazy blur. I remember the diagnosis only in the abstract, like the confused memory of a dream. People there told me about it, but I don't remember it myself, really. What I remember is feeling a sick sensation of fear and dread and disbelief. It was as if a comet had suddenly fallen from the sky and landed on top of me, squeezing out my thoughts and my breath. It was that horrific.

The thoughts in my brain ran in circles like a hamster on a wheel. Did I hear this correctly? The doctor said Glen is dying. He has Lou Gehrig's disease.

I knew what Lou Gehrig's disease was. I knew that it is 100 percent fatal. There is no treatment. There is no cure. I knew that if it were true, Glen's future — what little there would be of it — would be miserable for him.

CHAPTER TWENTY-TWO

GLEN'S VERSION OF THE DIAGNOSIS

Much later, Glen wrote about the events leading up to his diagnosis and the diagnosis itself. Using a specially adapted keyboard, Glen typed with his toes.

This is what he wrote:

Hello to all my church friends and family.

I am so honored and humbled by the sheer number of people who signed up to share emails with Vanessa and me and I am so blessed to have such a wonderful church family. You have shown us such love since my illness. You are always ready to pray or give physical support whenever we ask. A few of you I have about worn out, I have asked so much. I want to say thank you. If I may, I want to send you updates of my life and times every so often.

Vanessa said I have a dry sense of humor, I pray I never offend or hurt anyone. If I ever do, please let me know. I used to be a very private person, would not let anyone know my inner thoughts. That has changed since my illness. I don't know if it was being told I was going to die, or because I have lost almost all ability to take care of myself. Like I said, I never want to offend anyone, but I may say some honest and blunt things about how I feel. Now I am not going to tell you all my secrets, because I know you would NOT like me then, and I want you to like me, but if anyone has a question about my life, and how it has affected me, please ask. I do not ever want anyone to pity me or feel sorry for me, since my illness, we have been in a learning process. It has affected my family, of course. But I feel the one it has affected the most is Vanessa. I will give you a quick history lesson of the past eight years, plus.

I started choking.

The first time was on crackers and peanut butter. Vanessa tried the Heimlich. I am looking for something to fall onto to knock it loose. Vanessa is on the phone with 911, because I am turning blue, knowing any second I will pass out. Then through God's mercy, He allowed it to come up. So I went and had my throat checked. He did find my throat spasmed when he put the scope down, but he had no idea why.

With every symptom, every doctor, and with every test, the result was the same. "We can find nothing wrong with you." From the beginning, I forgot to tell you my body was extremely fatigued. It took everything I had just to get out of bed and move. By now, I am going crazy, because I know in my body that something is not right. Finally, on December 21, we got in to see a neurosurgeon. He comes in checks my reflexes, my ears, and throat. He said. Well, you do not need surgery. I think you have a nerve or a muscle problem. He turned my hands over and the muscle around my thumb had begun to deteriorate. He checked my reflexes on my right knee and my left leg would jump. When he looked at my tongue, it quivered.

He said, "I will call a neurologist and see if he can see you." So we got an appointment for the very next day, December 22, 2004. They called me into the room; Vanessa had to wait in the lobby. I had shorts on and a short sleeve shirt, a technician stuck monitor wires on my legs and arms, which were attached to a computer. They were about to do an EMG. Remember Vanessa is a nurse and knows exactly what happens during an EMG. You see my body is allergic to pain and when needles come at me, I get lightheaded. So the technician is up first. There I am lying on the table wires stuck on me that go to the computer. He starts on my right leg at the ankle. He makes a mark, measures up a certain distance and makes another mark. Then he shocked me with electricity and the current flowed between those two marks.

He measured and shocked several places up my leg. He moved then to my other leg and then to both arms. Some of the shocks felt about like an ant bite, not too bad. But some of them felt about like a wasp sting. Hurt. Now, remember that my body is allergic to pain.

He said the reason for the external shock was to see if current traveled the right nerve to the right place. So he's now done with all the "shock therapy," now it is the doctor's turn. He picks up a probe that I come to find out is a needle attached to a wire. This needle is four to five inches long. Do you remember what I said about needles? He went up both legs and arms, sticking that needle in me. Now to my surprise, I hardly felt the needle, must have been small diameter.

What I did feel was, with the needle in, he would have me move what was uncomfortable. Remember my quivering tongue? He went from the outside, below my chin under my tongue and buried that needle from the outside up into my tongue. To my amazement, I hardly felt it. Now the EMG was through. With all the wires removed, while he looks at the computer, the tech goes for Vanessa.

Finally, after two years of many symptoms, doctors, and tests, we were going to get a name to go with all my problems. Now I want you to get a picture in your mind. Remember what I said about no brains. I am sitting on the side of the table, legs hanging down. The doc is in a rolling exam chair straight in front of me, facing me. Vanessa is in a chair to my left, the doc's right. The doc very plainly and calmly said, "I am going to send you for a second opinion, but I feel confident that you have ALS, aka, Lou Gehrig's disease."

Now I have no clue what those words meant, they went right over my head. Remember Vanessa is a nurse. She grabbed her face and started to cry very hard. The doc turned to her and tried to console her. From her reaction, I knew it must be bad. Once back in the car, she explained to me that I had just been given a death sentence with no chance for survival.

But God and his awesome mercy . . .

Well I lied to you. I said I would take you through eight years, but I only made it two. Maybe I really am a big mouth. I plan to write again next week. You will enjoy that. It is about my three greatest battles. It is not what you think.

In Christ's Love, I write

Glen

My own reaction was not casual, accepting or even professional. I did not react with the grace and composure of a well-seasoned medical professional. I reacted exactly like a hysterical wife, which is what I was. This was one of those times, when my nursing expertise was a detriment. I did not have the reassuring comfort of ignorance. I knew too much.

I started crying. That alone was astonishing, especially to me. I have never been a person who cries. I get sad, but I usually did not cry. That was all about to change.

I cried and I cried. I couldn't stop. I cried almost continually for weeks after his diagnosis. I went to bed crying. I cried during the night and I cried in the morning. My eyes were red, my face perpetually puffy. I cried until I should have become dehydrated by the loss of so much water via tears.

I was protected to some extent by shock. Otherwise, I might have experienced a full-blown mental breakdown. My world became very small and very frightening. I could barely function; even to do the simplest of things. Everything that used to be easy became difficult, laborious, complicated. My mind was preoccupied with such horrible scenarios of the future that I could focus only on the simplest task. Wash this spoon. Fold the laundry. Brush my teeth. Even those I did with only partial attention. The dreadful reality was always in my mind. My formerly happy world where I felt safe, loved, and optimistic, had become a terrifying place. And yet, nothing changed in the world outside at all. The earth continued to spin as if nothing at all was wrong.

It seemed as if the world should take note of this profound tragedy. But it didn't seem to notice. Life refused to stop or even to slow down to accommodate my shattered world. It didn't pause a second to let me catch up, to catch my breath, to take it in, to come to terms with any of it.

All of this was so far outside of my ability to comprehend that I wandered through the day anxious, disbelieving, bewildered, confused and angry. There were none of the usual happy feelings associated with the holidays. I could not fathom that my soul mate, a man with such a giving, loving heart, could possibly have been so arbitrarily sentenced to death.

In the mornings, in the first half-instant before I became fully awake, I felt content for a nanosecond. A bad dream. None of it is real, I thought. For that brief instant, life was okay.

Then reality bore down with all the force of that streaking comet, crash-landing full-force on top of me.

I began to give myself mental marching orders.

Sit up. Put your feet on the floor. Stand up. Put one foot in front of the other. Move one foot. Move the other foot.

None of my life's previous priorities seemed to matter. Who cared what I made for dinner, what I wore that day, what flowers I planted or which book I checked out of the library?

The earth continued to spin as it always had. Life around me kept doing what life always does, expecting me to do what I have always done. It did not matter how difficult the circumstances, how physically and emotionally distraught I was, the world and its requirements of me kept chugging along as methodically as a conveyor belt. My nursing commitments are there. The car needs gas. The laundry needs doing. Meals need to be cooked. Glen needs care. The utility bills still need to be paid and emails and phone calls returned.

Oh, and it is Christmastime. How un-merry I felt. But there were obligations. There were gifts, last-minute baking, Merry Christmas visits and calls to make.

I felt alone in my cataclysmic circumstance. So far, only Glen and I knew what was going on. Unlike myself, Glen did have the reassurance of ignorance. I'm sure he understood on an intellectual level, but the reality had not sunk in. He remained largely uninformed of the magnitude of his reality. I did not wish to produce more angst for him by spelling out the excruciating details. Knowing his future would not have changed the prognosis in the least.

Chapter twenty-three

TELLING THE FAMILY

We needed to tell the family, but we did not want to ruin Christmas for them. To this day, Thanksgiving and Christmas holidays are so painful that we choose to celebrate in the most non-traditional ways we can think of.

We did call Rev. Don Davis of First Assembly of God, our church pastor, and tell him. We asked that he not tell any other church members until after we were able to talk to Jacob in Iraq. We were afraid for him to hear the news first from someone else. In this high-tech world, information can move at the speed of light.

The day Glen was diagnosed we told our daughter, Glen's sister, Brenda, and her husband Ronnie Berry. When Glen was about middle school age, he was the one who gave his sister in marriage to Ronnie. They were all very close.

We told Jacob when he called on Christmas Eve 2004 to wish us a Merry Christmas.

It was difficult to talk to Jacob about his father's diagnosis from the other side of the planet. From so far away, I could not see his face or wrap my arms around him. At first, Jacob didn't understand what I was trying to tell him. But he surmised by my tone that it was a terrible thing.

"I was in Iraq and I had a lot of things on my mind. I didn't completely understand what ALS was, but I could tell from my mother's reaction that it was something bad," Jacob said. "She's a nurse, so she would know. She's usually very calm about things."

We waited until after Christmas to inform the extended family.

After the holidays, we visited Glen's other sister, Mary Ann Allen, fourteen years his elder. "I knew something was up when they all came together to see me," Mary Ann said.

"They told me, but it didn't fully sink in. I couldn't believe that Glen would really die."

Mary Ann, Brenda, and pretty much all of the family felt the same way. "I just kept thinking that it had to be a mistake. It just had to be," Brenda said.

That sense of shock and denial prevailed throughout the family, then and for a long time afterward.

To soften the news, in every conversation, we placed a heavy emphasis on the fact that we would be getting a second opinion, and that this all was probably a terrible mistake. We were convinced that the doctors had to be wrong. They had made a mistake. It happens. We all believed that this was some crazy mistake. Our brains could not process such unthinkable information.

Or, even if it were true that Glen was sick, we figured it had to be some different, treatable, non-terminal disease. Once we got it all straightened out, we'd start a proper treatment and everyone's lives would continue, as they should.

Even if that worst worst-case scenario were true — that Glen really and truly had ALS — we were sure that God would intervene and heal him.

We started praying for that and we asked others to pray for Glen. His name was placed onto prayer lists all over the country. The reality still hadn't sunk in. Every one of us was convinced that Glen would recover.

We held onto that dream for as long as we possibly could.

"I never, ever thought Daddy was going to die," our daughter said. She wrote her father an email not long before he died, describing her eagerness for God's healing and her expectation that her father would give her one of his wonderful bear hugs again.

Glen himself acted as if he didn't take his situation too seriously. He shrugged it off with jokes when he told his friend, Bobby.

Glen took Bobby behind the bank for a private talk.

"Neither one of us wanted to believe it," Bobby said. "When he told me, he just laughed it off. Glen cracked jokes about living long enough to draw all his social security, about how he'd be sitting in his rocking chair and laughing about it. He just brushed it off.

"None of it made any sense," he said. "We had all gone to school together, grown up together, gone to proms together. Glen was a regular guy. A good guy. Things like this don't happen to regular guys, not guys I went to school with. Not a really, good guy like Glen. It was surreal."

CHAPTER TWENTY-FOUR

SECOND OPINION: HOUSTON

We still held on to the possibility that the second opinion would quash the erroneous diagnosis. Jacob came back from Iraq in January. In February 2005, Glen, our children and I went to Houston, Texas, to the ALS Clinic for the second opinion. The clinic was the leading research center in the south for patients with ALS.

Glen endured another grueling battery of tests. He repeated the EMG and had a spinal tap. Then we all heard for a second time that he had ALS and was going to die. The second official pronouncement of Glen's death sentence was delivered with all the warmth of an automobile mechanic talking about a bad fuel pump.

Maybe it wasn't as insensitive as it felt to me. Or maybe it was delivered so matter-of-factly because doctors fear if they show too much sensitivity, the horror will come down too hard on the family. Then the family will freak out and go berserk right there in the office. I don't think there's any possible way we could have been more freaked out than we already were.

"The first time we went to Houston in 2005 was when it started to sink in," Jacob said. "We were in a room with about a dozen doctors. When you're in a room full of doctors all saying it, you start to get that it's serious."

These were the doctor's words:

"Glen has ALS, Lou Gehrig's disease."

"Glen is in the early stages."

"Glen has the rare form of Bulbar-Onset ALS, which begins at the top of the body."

"Paralysis will come in the final stage."

"We don't know what causes ALS."

"There is no cure for ALS."

"There is no real treatment for ALS."

"Life expectancy averages three years."

"You should get your affairs in order."

"End of report. Any questions?"

The hopeful report we had counted on had not come. I don't really remember who said what, but what I heard was this — Glen dying. No hope. Time running out. Get affairs in order immediately.

We traveled back home. We were exhausted and in shock. We still did not believe it could be true, but now we were less certain of our disbelief. I was devastated all over again, I was reeling and robotic. Hope was gone. Being a nurse was an agonizing blessing. I had the training and expertise to manage his physical needs. I knew where to go and where to look for information and assistance with his care. But the flip side of that experience brought the knowledge of just how debilitated he would become from this cruel disease. I knew it all far better than he did. I did not particularly wish to share more information with him. The knowledge of his grim future wouldn't change a thing.

Worse, this was not some random patient, from whom I could professionally detach.

This was my husband.

When I am nursing others, I can keep an objective distance. That is essential for effective care. Emotional attachment can be detrimental.

But this was Glen, my life partner, the father of my children. His health and happiness and his life felt somehow connected to my own.

We came home with information overload. My priority became his care, which soon became a time-consuming array of tasks. I shifted into nurse-protector mode.

After his diagnosis, we were directed to occupational therapy, physical therapy and counseling to guide us. I moved mechanically through the gamut of professionals, neurologists, speech therapists, physical therapists, dietitians and counselors. Each specialist tested him, documented his status and established a baseline of his abilities or lack of abilities at that point.

Chapter twenty-five

MELTDOWN

By now, I had begun to operate day in and day out in a chronic state of shock. I tried to be strong, to maintain a positive attitude, and to draw heavily on my spiritual faith. I was convinced we would receive a miracle of divine healing.

But I was secretly terrified.

During one Houston trip, my façade of fortitude collapsed like a tattered beach umbrella in a hurricane. Glen and I had just celebrated a wedding anniversary. I feared it would be our last. We went back into our counselor's office when my emotions gushed forth, surprising all three of us. I burst into tears. Glen sat silently. I stood behind him, wrapped my arms around him and sobbed as if my heart was breaking. All of my secret fears fell out of my mouth and out of my eyes. I stood emotionally naked in my counselor's office. I told Glen how terrified I was that he wouldn't be around for our next anniversary. In spite of our denial, we knew that we could lose him at any moment.

The counselor was taken aback by my unexpected outburst.

"I have never seen you react like this," she said. "You have always been so positive."

Of course, she was right. Most of my tears had been shed in private.

The counselor, realizing how much more upset I was than I had been letting on, urged me to consider antidepressants, to soften the intensity of my emotions. She also urged me to focus on the present moment and to celebrate life each day. I agreed to both. We would embrace each day, and that day only. We would not worry about the next day. But we never stopped praying for a miracle.

The antidepressants did enable me to function without strong emotional outbursts, and I needed to be able to function.

Because his lower body had not yet been affected and his remaining level of function was fair, Glen was deemed a good candidate for trial studies.

We made three trips back to Houston. We were the recipient of people's gracious generosity every step of the way.

We discovered two organizations most people probably don't know about. We discovered Pilots for Christ and Angel Flight.

Pilots for Christ and Angel Flight organizations are a sort of loosely assembled groups of matchmaking non-profits that help arrange free air transportation for people who must travel far for specialized medical treatment. The organizations connect people who have a compelling need for transportation, but cannot afford it, with individual humanitarian pilots willing to provide free flights. In some cases, other compelling human needs are served, such as transportation to visit a hospitalized family member, or transportation helping in time of emergencies or disasters such as the aftermath of Hurricane Katrina and Hurricane Sandy.

Patients must be medically stable and able to stand and sit unassisted and cannot be emergency patients. These humanitarian missions are made possible by pilots who volunteer their time, their skills, and the funds required for aircraft operating expenses. Many pilots provide the flights in their own personal aircraft, although some do so using rented aircraft. Pilots must usually meet certain minimum flight experience requirements before they are allowed to command an air mission. They also receive training on the special procedures required for these flights . The pilots are strictly pilots, not medical personnel.

They absorb all the costs of the missions. Pilots' expenses are generally tax-deductible as a "gift-in-kind" donation, and the flights provide a satisfying purpose to the pilot's accumulation of required air miles.

The patients initiate a request for transportation from their home to the clinic they need to go, with information about the situation and number traveling. Pilot volunteers then check the mission list and can assign themselves to a mission that is appropriate to their aircraft and schedule.

There are numerous similar organizations, depending on where in the United States or the world you may be. The one that helped us provides services in the Southeast, throughout Georgia, Alabama, Mississippi, Tennessee and the Carolinas.

Pilots for Christ and Angel Flight organizations work in tandem with a similar group of volunteers on the ground, called "Ground Angels." They help transport patients after they arrive at their destination.

Arranging for an Angel Flight is a complicated, time-consuming matter. Because the pilots typically have regular day jobs and lives of their own, scheduling requires a great deal of advance planning.

We needed to request and submit our destination and our exact travel dates as far in advance as possible. Sometimes the trip could be a little convoluted and piecemeal. It could be just a little bit like hitchhiking on the highway, but with airplanes in the sky. We almost never had the same pilot. We might have one pilot traveling to our destination and a different one traveling home. We might have one plane and pilot who could take us partway, then a different plane and pilot picked us up and took us the rest of the way. Sometimes we traveled with other patients. After we arrived, there were volunteer "Ground Angels," who took us to where we needed to go from there.

Because Glen had ALS, some pilots were a little reluctant to accept him. They were not sure he qualified as a patient who could sit and stand on his own. We had to assure the pilots that Glen was able to walk.

We were immensely grateful for each one of those volunteers. But we began to dread the trips, not so much because of the travel, but because of the harsh dose of ALS reality thrust into our faces at the clinic. We waited in the clinic lobby with other ALS patients and their families. All were in varying degrees of the disease, the sight of which ripped off any protective denial we still had. Our grim destiny was sitting right there in front of our faces.

One day, another patient in the room where we were waiting began to choke in that horrifying way that only an ALS patient chokes. Every face in the room instantly froze in horror. Even I was horrified. But that is the universal response to ALS choking.

Neither of us could endure the sight of people suffering the later stages of the disease. We could see our future selves in them. Instead of gaining strength from visiting with others in similar situations, we found it frightening and demoralizing. For us, it instilled a sense of near-hopelessness. That is not to say every patient and his family would have the same reaction. It is important for each person to listen to his own heart about what is right for them.

There were many trials or studies open to us. Some focused on antibiotics, some involved hormones, and others were experimental drug studies. There were studies with stem cells. Doctors told us about some experimental Chinese procedures performed directly on the brain. The medications involved would not cost us anything. The sheer array of studies was mind-boggling. There were complicated non-optional stipulations for becoming part of a trial. First, being in a trial study meant frequent travel between Alabama and Texas for monitoring. That travel would be dictated by the needs of the study, not the needs of the patient. Glen would become a human guinea pig.

I was a little uneasy. Some of the trials seemed risky. At this point, Glen was very ill, but his quality of life was still good. The patient would endure various treatments, with no assurance that he would improve — or that he wouldn't get worse. I could not believe we were considering some of these strange trials, but when you are desperate, you will consider anything.

We weighed the pros and cons. We considered whether his transformation from patient to guinea pig, with no guarantee that he could retain any quality of life, would be worth it. We traveled back to Houston several times. Each visit was more about supplying data than treating Glen. During each visit, his physical abilities were evaluated for any degeneration, but for the time being, he seemed to have settled into a holding pattern.

In the end, we declined the trial studies. We didn't want to risk losing the quality of life Glen had. Each circumstance, each patient is unique. What might be right for one might not be right for another. This was the right decision for us.

We didn't go back to Houston after that.

Such horrifying life-and-death decisions began to occur with increasing frequency in our lives.

It was just a few months later that Glen began seeing Dr. George McCullars.

Chapter twenty-six

ANTIBIOTICS

We searched everywhere for reassurance. We pored over one Biblical scripture after another, seeking guidance. We posted scriptures related to Christ's healing power all over the house to reinforce a positive outlook. Meanwhile, I researched everything I could find to learn of any new treatments or trials under consideration.

So far, the only drug approved by the U.S. Food and Drug Administration to treat ALS is riluzole (Rilutek®). But it only prolongs life by two to three months and does nothing to relieve symptoms.

I had already managed to convince Glen to let me do all the research on the Internet. I did not want an overload of frightening information adding to his burden.

It turned out that a local man in town had read an article in an out-of-town newspaper about a man who had been misdiagnosed with ALS for 7 years. It turned out that the man actually had Lyme disease.

The article talked about George McCullars, a physician and a Ph.D., who specializes in Lyme disease. Lyme disease has symptoms very similar to those of Amyotrophic Lateral Sclerosis, but is not necessarily fatal. Lyme disease is an infectious disease caused by bacteria of the Borrelia genus, carried by ticks. If treated early with antibiotics, there is a good chance of recovery, although delays create significant difficulties in treatment and can worsen into conditions that are much harder to treat. The other man tested positive for Lyme disease and began antibiotic treatments.

There is no true test for ALS. A diagnosis is achieved by an exhaustive battery of tests and the exclusion of all other possible causes. Other diseases mimic the symptoms of ALS, and some are treatable.

A copy of that newspaper article ended up in the hands of some people in our town. They then shared it with our daughter Marcy, who was reluctant to share it with us for fear of giving us false hope.

But eventually she gave us the article. Dr. McCullars practiced in Mobile, so he was not very far away from us. I thought it couldn't hurt to check into the possibility. Glen was reluctant at first. But I urged him. What did he have to lose?

Twice already, he had been given a death sentence. It took some convincing, but he finally relented. I called immediately and got an appointment for the next day due to a fortuitous cancellation.

Glen began seeing George McCullars, MD, Ph.D. He did believe that Glen had Lyme disease and put him on antibiotics. Within a few weeks, Glen responded. The rapid progression of the disease simply stopped. It stalled out. The damage and symptoms already present didn't go away, but his symptoms stopped getting worse. We were overjoyed.

All the symptoms of muscle weakness, loss of dexterity of his hands, extreme fatigue, difficulty speaking and swallowing and the choking that he already had remained.

He still choked a lot, his muscles were still weak, he still grew weary quickly, but he was able to get out of the house and have some kind of a life. For most of his illness, people who did not know he had ALS thought he had suffered a stroke. His arms and hands were losing function, but he could still walk, and did so with a shuffling gait almost to the very end.

The medical community remains unconvinced that antibiotics could be a valid treatment for ALS. There have been anecdotal instances of improvement with antibiotics. However, in some other cases, antibiotics have seemed to make symptoms worse. Any patient should consult with his doctors. There will need to be much more investigation before the medical community knows how a particular antibiotic can be beneficial to any category of ALS patient.

I can only say what happened with one patient. For whatever reason, the antibiotic treatment did help Glen, for which we are very grateful. The antibiotics were a Godsend for about five years. They seemed to hold back the progression of his disease for as long as he took them.

After he had taken them for five years, he was taken off antibiotics and his symptoms began to worsen rapidly again. He was immediately put back on antibiotics, but the second time they did not help.

We all went back and forth, and around and around, about what we believed or didn't believe. We desperately wanted to believe that Glen did have Lyme disease or some other disease.

At that time, we honestly didn't know, but the antibiotics seemed to help, and that was all that mattered to us. An autopsy after Glen's death confirmed that he did in fact have ALS.

Glen learned to adjust so that he could still have some kind of a life. Just as all of us do as we age and certain things grow more difficult for us, Glen adapted. He learned to maneuver his body, to shift his weight, to use his forearms to do all manner of things for himself. He just did them differently. Later on, he used all sorts of assistive tools, some designed for stroke victims, some he designed for himself. Later he became adept at using his feet to do all sorts of things people do with their hands.

PART FOUR

AFFAIRS IN ORDER

CHAPTER TWENTY-SEVEN

MAKING CHANGES

We still did not believe he would die. We believed — as people in denial do — that Glen would never succumb to whatever disease he had. We still had doubts about whether he really had Lou Gehrig's disease. For a very long time, our acceptance of Glen's illness refused to allow room for death. We were convinced he would recover; we simply did not know when that would be.

Whether we believed he was truly dying or not, Glen was sick and needed our care. Antibiotics aside, we knew on some level that Glen's life existed in a precarious state of borrowed time. We knew that any remission the antibiotics provided could end abruptly at any moment.

The whole family had always operated extremely well as a team. Now the family buckled down like never before.

"We never just sat around and talked about how we should do this or that, or who should do what. We just got up and did what needed to be done. We are doers, not talkers. We've always been that way," our daughter said. "Whenever something needed to be done, we just banded together and did it as a family. It was just another Maholovich challenge. We coped the way we always coped with everything," she continued, with a shrug that suggested we wouldn't know any other way.

It would be a long time before Glen fully accepted any more help than he absolutely had to, even from other members of the family. He allowed me to help, but he wasn't happy about it. And he sometimes tried to hide just how difficult things were for him.

Glen's strength and dexterity were gone. Upper-body paralysis had begun to overtake him. The choking, the twitching, the muscle weakness, the voice change, the difficulty speaking and swallowing were becoming routine. He became more fatigued with even less exertion.

I have been a nurse for more than thirty years, but none of my training or experience made it easier to know that Glen had ALS. When it is someone you love deeply, someone you have loved nearly all of your life, the experience becomes personal, with an excruciatingly difficult learning curve. The antidepressants I started taking controlled the intensity of my emotions just enough to do the things I needed to do on a daily basis. But's that's about all.

Our pleasant small-town life became the negative inverse of what it had been. We had been comfortable empty nesters, well settled in our familiar routines.

That had to change.

I began to incorporate Glen's chores and duties into my schedule, to compensate for those things he could no longer do. I let him instruct me to do certain things, minor repairs around the house that I had never done before.

I cooked, cleaned, shopped, did the laundry, took out the trash. I ran errands he used to run. There were certain things I could not do. At the time of Glen's diagnosis, we were living in Glen's sprawling childhood home on State Line Road, the one that separates Florida from Alabama. The house fronts acreage of fields and pastures that had to be bush-hogged with a tractor.

He was a much larger and stronger person than I was. Or he had been, before he became ill. He outweighed me by 100 pounds. That strength and size had enabled him to perform tasks that my petite body would never be able to do, no matter how much I wanted to.

Glen could no longer mow a five-acre lawn; neither could he bush-hog 20-odd acres of pasture behind the house. I could never have physically managed that and if I could have, I could never have found time to do it.

Glen was having difficulty operating machinery. It would soon be a safety issue. I was working full-time, doing the household and family chores, as I had always done, but now I was performing many of the tasks that he used to do and increasingly caring for him.

Sometimes a family member or close friend stepped in to help with things I could not do. Other times, we had to make drastic changes to accommodate his illness. Meanwhile, I worked full-time as a nurse.

Glen started talking about selling our home and property.

I knew this had to happen, but it still broke my heart. We had just recently completed the work on a ten-year, do-it-yourself renovation. It had been such a long, hard project that I wanted to sit back and enjoy the results. I did not look forward to moving.

We had been told to get our affairs in order, so we did. Immediately after the worst of the shock had passed, we began to arrange for Glen's retirement, for which we were not at all prepared. I continued to work, but Glen simply could not. Glen retired on June 24, 2005, six months after his diagnosis. It was nearly twenty years earlier than he expected to retire.

We began to make our way through the labyrinth of legal and financial paperwork issues that needed to be sorted out. Glen immediately began transferring things over into my name. Then he took me to business school. When he received his diagnosis, Glen began to worry about my palpable aversion to handling finances. I detest — I cannot emphasize that enough — I detest financial and business matters. With his banking expertise, he was a natural. In our marriage, we had fallen into our comfortable routines, and business had not been my forte.

He began to have me handle business matters as he walked me through them. He had me make the phone calls for any business situation. He patiently set out to teach me how to handle all of our financial affairs. He was clearly worried about how I would manage without him.

One day he and I were seated at opposite sides of his desk. I had been on the phone with someone about insurance or banking or something. After I hung up, he looked at me with a look of deep relief and heaved an audible sigh.

"All right, I've done it," he said. "You actually sounded like you knew what you were talking about." And by this time, I did know.

I still detest finances, but at least I learned how to handle them.

Just in case I forgot, I suppose, Glen left me with itemized lists and information about how to handle various problems and who to consult if I had a problem.

Later I wrote letters to the people he put on his list. One of them sent me back every one of his phone numbers plus his email addresses. And if I needed to, I would turn to them, mostly because Glen trusted them. That was good enough for me.

Chapter twenty-eight

FINANCIAL IMPACT

We were in no way financially prepared for such an early retirement, let alone the added expenses of major medical care. We had all the same financial commitments as before, minus one income. Glen cashed in his retirement and we knew that we would have to sell whatever we could.

The Muscular Dystrophy Association is a phenomenal resource for ALS patients. Together with The Lewin Group, they conducted and published a study of the annual cost per patient for three common neuromuscular disorders. ALS turned out to be the most expensive. The study was published online July 8, 2013, in the journal *Muscle & Nerve*.

The study calculated that a patient will feel the financial cost of ALS at a conservative cost of $63,700 a year, only a part of which would be covered by insurance or Medicare. That number is an average and each situation is different, of course, but even the study's authors believe the number they presented to be lower than the true cost. To put the numbers into perspective, the median household income for Alabama residents about that time was slightly more than $51,000. The annual financial burden of the disease exceeded that by $12,700.

A wonderful advantage of living in a tiny community is that when everyone knows everyone, everyone cares a little bit more about everyone else. We were extremely fortunate. The community came to our rescue in so many ways.

People held fund raisers for Glen, which enabled us to pay off loans we had. People at the bank donated their vacation days and time off to Glen, so that he received a paycheck until his disability took effect. Typically, it takes two years for a person to receive a disability classification. The life expectancy for an ALS patient is just two to three years, meaning the patient could easily be dead before he was ever declared disabled. Thanks to the efforts of another man with ALS, that wait is now waived.

Without help from so many different volunteers, friends and strangers alike, we could not have made it. It was very kind and generous for people to do that. For us, however, accepting such help was humbling. It was an entirely unfamiliar experience for us. We had to learn to be okay with receiving help. That was hard.

With Glen's retirement came the issue of health insurance coverage. This happened before the Affordable Care Act, so at the time insurance plans ran the gamut as to what they cost and what they covered. Glen was enrolled in Medicare due to his disability, but he needed more coverage. We began to research insurance options. We discovered that if we moved into Alabama, he could receive better coverage at a more affordable rate. We were still living on the Florida side of the road.

Glen began to research places to live in Alabama. We both knew it would not be wise to go far from family and friends. We knew that their support and help would be vital as the disease progressed.

We owned a small 1940s cottage-style house in Atmore. Our original plan — before we knew that Glen would need to retire — had been to fix it up and resell it, or flip it as an investment. The location was ideal. It was an older home, but its structure was sound. All it needed was some sprucing up. And that had been our combined forte. What we had not anticipated was that the housing market would crash at exactly that time. Before that, houses were selling quickly at good prices. Our timing could not have been worse.

Our only option was to renovate the little cottage and rent it out. But he was in no condition to work on the house himself. So he subbed out the work and hired others. He called them his "Team of Misfits." They were friends of his, each of whom had some physical impediment — a bad back or bad knees — but together they managed to do it. Glen oversaw each phase of the renovation.

Still, he hated standing back and watching. The thought of slowing down, doing less, was against his nature. It just felt wrong to him. In the past he could jump into a project, work his day job and work long hours after that. Now he had to learn to pace himself, which was altogether a new experience for him.

Less than one month after his retirement, he was outside trying to fortify the house for Hurricane Dennis, which was headed our way. He still hadn't adjusted to slowing down. Some of the family were staying with us, and all of us were very nervous when Glen went outside before the storm to hook up a generator to the power box outside. Later, he went out into the eye of the storm to put fuel in the generator. We all were terrified he would be killed. We watched with alarm as I repeatedly told Glen that no one knew the duration of the storm's eye. It didn't matter. Fortunately, Dennis made landfall July 10 to the east of us as a weakened storm.

CHAPTER TWENTY-NINE

THE HOUSEBOAT

Meanwhile, Glen had his heart set on living on or near the water. He started looking for living options. Both of us loved the water. It had been a dream for us to live near the water, eventually. Now Glen was determined to bump up the schedule. He started thinking about living on a houseboat.

Glen came across an area on the Tensaw River across the county line in Alabama. Specifically, he found a place called Lower Bryant's landing that was designated for houseboats. There was a houseboat community already established there. He found some houseboats for sale. Glen began lining up his arguments in favor of moving there. It would still be in Alabama, where insurance was cheaper for more coverage.

Glen continued his campaign to convince me to consider living on a houseboat. He meticulously lined up each argument, like some carefully engineered line of dominoes. Then he presented them to me.

I was skeptical, but I was also open-minded. By this time, I would have done anything in my power to add a moment of joy to Glen's life. If he had wanted to move to India, I would have made that move. So when he approached me, though, I didn't say yes right away, I did agree to consider it.

I had no real-world understanding of living on a houseboat, which may have been the reason I was hesitant. My only image of houseboat living came from old movies and TV. What I envisioned was the shoeless, backwoodsy lifestyle depicted by the Tammy movies and television show. In those, the homespun character Tammy pushed her ramshackle, hillbilly-style houseboat along the river with a great big stick. That was not the least bit appealing to me. It sounded like lots of hard work with few rewards and no household comforts.

Maybe we aren't "dress for dinner" people; but we aren't barefoot hicks, either.

When we went to look at some places along the river, I discovered that my mental image of houseboat living needed some revision. Lower Bryant's landing was a fully developed community on the Tensaw River in Alabama. If ever there were a serene and relaxing setting, the Tensaw River is it. It is unspoiled and woodsy and feels deliciously isolated from the chaos of everyday life. We explored all the landings up and down what I called the "river road." There were many, but we kept coming back to one in particular.

It felt safe, protected and populated with friendly people. It was ideally suited for families, which was a requirement for us so that our grandchildren could visit.

It truly was isolated, out in the middle of nowhere. There is one gas station and some old historical homes in the general area, but as rustic as it appeared, as much as it screamed out "roughing it," it turned out to have every convenience we needed. There was trash collection, cable television, Internet access, and mail and UPS delivery. During the summertime, an old-fashioned ice cream truck made regular runs down the dirt roads. There was a hidden gem of a restaurant, The Stage Coach, across from a gas station, which later became significant to us. While Glen could eat very few things, he could eat ice cream. The Stage Coach is where he became well known for eating ice cream by the plateful.

It's true that mobile phone calls were tricky. On at least one occasion, we know that Glen left a voicemail message for someone in town who did not receive it for three days. But we managed. We found we could pick up a signal, if we walked down to a particular spot out near the road and stood in a particular position. But we also had a regular phone.

It was quite a long drive from there to Atmore where I worked, but I could make that drive, I reasoned. There were cute little cottage-style houseboats lined up along the road. The front doors faced the road, and each was accessed by a small wooden bridge to the home. The backside of the houseboat faced the peaceful river. The houseboats themselves floated entirely over deep water, securely anchored and stationary.

I thought, okay, I can do this. I can live here. I felt safe and comfortable in the little river community. It took a few months for the sale of our State Line road property. But we found a little houseboat that we could afford and snapped it up.

Moving from a rambling 2,000-square-feet home to a boat with only 700 square feet of living space required considerable downsizing. So, we sold and stored most of our possessions.

It was quite a drastic change for us. It was a boat, after all. Our living space shrank from sprawling house to that of a large hotel suite or a small apartment. But it was just the two of us.

The change wasn't bad. In fact, it was a respite. It was another world for us. A haven that held the awfulness of the disease at bay, somewhere else, out there in some alternate universe. The houseboat floated over the deep waters of the Tensaw River, surrounded on the three sides overlooking the river by a wooden deck with many holes designed to hold fishing poles. At one end of the deck, there was a diving board. We could boat and ride jet skis — and one day, an inadvertent Jet Ski tumble by visitors in front of Glen provided him no end of mirth. A wonderful screened-in porch at the back of the houseboat overlooked the deck and the river. Our houseboat became our floating sanctuary. It was small, but perfect for us.

Glen's spirits soared. He became excited. The move had given him something new and different to think about. He could fish, he could boat, and he could watch the sunrise and set over the still waters from his deck.

It's practically impossible to be stressed living on a quiet river. The gently rolling water and the soothing breezes won't permit it. I watched the tension drain out of Glen. Seeing Glen happy helped to alleviate my own stress. That alone made our decision worth it.

However, our houseboat honeymoon came to an abrupt end. Or rather, a temporary interruption. Just a few months after settling in, we discovered our little home was infested with mold. Molds are fungi needed to break down dead material and recycle nutrients in the environment, but can also pose a serious health risk, especially to someone whose health is already compromised. Exposure to some molds can result in chronic headaches and fatigue, eye irritation, fever, and nose and throat irritation. Glen was already so ill, and the mold most certainly would aggravate his symptoms.

The mold needed to be re-mediated and the houseboat renovated. We had no choice but to move out and start one more renovation. Glen was unable to perform the work himself, but supervised every move by the crew who did it.

In life, sometimes things work out coincidentally well. As grim as many of these circumstances were, we felt divinely protected all along the way. I suppose it's easier to see the blessings along the way if you're looking for them. And we were looking for them.

As it happened, our little cottage in town was still unoccupied. We were able to stay in the cottage until we could move back into our beloved newly renovated houseboat. And when we moved back to the houseboat, we were able to rent out the little cottage in town.

CHAPTER THIRTY

HOUSEBOAT TRACHEOTOMY

During the period of renovation, when the boat was mostly stripped of furniture, Glen was nearly the recipient of an unwanted ballpoint pen tracheotomy.

Glen and Bobby decided to spend the night on the houseboat so they could do some fishing. By this time, Glen could not utilize his upper body much, but he could hunch forward and inward and maneuver his weight in such a way that he could use a combination of his forearms and his feet to grasp the fishing pole. There was never a time when Glen allowed his disease to rob him of his life's pleasures if he could figure out some way around it. He was rapidly becoming skilled at using his feet to do remarkable things most people do with their hands.

Glen was sleeping on an air mattress and Bobby was in a sleeping bag. Before they went to the river, we warned Bobby about Glen's choking. He had never witnessed it firsthand. But whenever the subject came up, Glen joked about it, so that when Glen actually choked when they were alone on the houseboat, Bobby was surprised by its intensity.

It happened in the middle of the night.

They spent the day crabbing and fishing and then settled in to sleep. Around two in the morning, Glen started choking. It was so horrific that Bobby forgot what we told him and started to panic. "I didn't know what to do," Bobby said. "I went over to start doing the Heimlich maneuver. But Glen stopped me. He motioned to me that it would not work."

Glen's choking was getting worse.

Bobby became desperate. If the Heimlich maneuver wouldn't help, he had no idea what else to do. Then he remembered all of those dramatic television shows about ballpoint pen tracheotomies. In those, a bystander makes a deep cut in the neck through to the windpipe of a person who can't breathe and then inserts into that the barrel of a ballpoint pen through which air can be drawn into the lungs. Bobby decided that was what he had to do. He would perform a ballpoint-pen-tracheotomy. He began frantically searching everywhere for a pen and something to cut with. As he searched, he explained his plan to Glen. That's when Glen panicked.

His eyes grew wide. His face became white and he was clearly terrified. He began feverishly gesturing, motioning, and indicating in every way possible that a tracheotomy was a decidedly bad idea.

"Luckily, ya'll had taken all the sharp instruments out of the house," Bobby said, "Because Glen would not have been strong enough to stop me once I started."

Only later did Bobby learn that Glen's choking spasm would have run its course and end on its own. Bobby had no idea his plan to perform a makeshift tracheotomy on Glen would have been disastrous. "It would have been bad if I'd been trying to save his life, but accidentally killed him with a ballpoint pen," Bobby said.

CHAPTER THIRTY-ONE

MUD WRESTLING

I had my own adventures with Glen at the river. Storms are common along the Gulf Coast. While we lived there, the river would occasionally crest, causing the area to flood. We usually evacuated to Glen's sister's house. The boat, which was on higher ground, would float, but the roadway would be underwater. The area flooded three times during the time we lived there.

Generally, we made the necessary preparations to secure the houseboat and if the storm was bad, we evacuated. Once, just before one was due to arrive; Glen decided he needed to turn off the water to the houseboat, which had to be accomplished near the road at the top of a steep, sloping bank.

I am not quite sure how it happened, but apparently Glen stumbled and the next thing I knew he was on the ground in the mud. The ALS had taken such a toll on his muscles that by this point he was no more able to right himself than an upturned turtle would be.

I rushed out and tried to pull him up. Although he had lost some of his former athletic bulk, he was still a hundred pounds heavier than I was. Ordinarily I couldn't help him up from a fall on my own; I hoped that with just the right leverage I might be able to pull him up. But the steeply sloping bank was slick with mud and soon I tumbled into the mud as well.

We began to roll around in the mud.

It was just the two of us, maneuvering, struggling to get our footing or, for at least one of us, to get a foothold. We tumbled, wrestled, and rolled. I was getting mud in my mouth and my hair and all over my clothes. So was Glen. After struggling a while, it began to occur to me that I might not be able to get him up. He was about 200 pounds of dead weight, with atrophied muscles that could not assist me. These were definitely not the best of circumstances.

I began to panic. My thoughts swirled in my head.

What if I can't get him up? I don't think I can get him up.

I drafted scenarios in my brain. After a long while, some guy walking his dog — it is always some guy walking his dog — would find us, all wet and muddy and starved to death on the riverbank. He'd wonder why the heck those crazy people were out here in the first place and why on earth they had stayed out here. Why didn't the fools just go back inside the houseboat, instead of starving to death on the riverbank?

By this time, I was exhausted, filthy, terrified and completely spent. It seemed like we were rolling over, and over, and fighting and struggling to get up for a very long time. I knew that no one would come. No one could see us. We were in a sort of deep ditch, difficult to see from the road, even if there was traffic, but there wasn't any.

Finally, after what seemed like hours, but was probably just a few minutes, we managed to kind of roll, and push and pull, shove, and struggle to our feet. I can only imagine what a ridiculous sight it would have been for anyone who did see us.

Eventually the houseboat renovation was finished, and we moved back in. We were in our pleasant sanctuary again.

Friends dropped by. The children and the grandchildren came to swim, fish, and boat. Sometimes we talked, played cards or just relaxed, and sometimes we fed the fish in the pond that Glen had created for me at the front of the house. The fish knew when feeding time arrived and they swam up and waited. Before long, it became everyone's private island of serenity, a place where the grim reality wasn't as heavy a weight. The breezes off the water kept us comfortable. Across the road on the higher dry land, we parked our boat and cars. In the river road community, everyone looked out for one another. We checked in on each other.

It is so easy to become almost shell-shocked from the perpetual stress of standing guard over another person's life. I found an unanticipated creative outlet. By designing and decorating our floating cottage, I experienced respite from the reality that my husband was dying. I am not a professional decorator, but I have always had a good eye and an artistic flair for it. I enjoyed shopping for items for the house and then planning, designing and arranging them to establish a pleasant mood and create a new look. It was a temporary escape from my workday world of nursing, where mistakes can be disastrous. It was a break from my caretaker duties where mistakes could be dangerous to my husband. For a caretaker, every tiny moment of respite is essential for sanity.

The best part of decorating was that it held no inherent life-threatening hazards. It was a relief to be able to do just one thing that did not require my constant vigilance. I could relax and feel at ease. That was something that, by this point, I had not been able to do for a long time. So what if I painted the walls some crazy, weird color? Walls can be repainted. Lives aren't lost because of a poor paint color choice.

We only got to live on the houseboat for about a year and a half, but it was a year and a half of wonderful memories. We sold it after we moved back to town, and if I thought that I could handle the painful memories I would buy it back. For now, I can't.

CHAPTER THIRTY-TWO

MORE ADAPTING

Glen despised being dependent. Self-reliance had been his code from birth. He had moments of deep frustration, especially at times when he knew exactly what he wanted to accomplish but no matter how hard he tried, he could not make his body do it. During one of the times the river flooded, we stayed with Glen's sister Mary Ann.

In his heart and mind, Glen was still the man whose entire life had been built around his athletic and physical abilities. Just as many people in middle age still feel eighteen on the inside, Glen still felt like the superman he had always been.

Until then, we had never realized the number of products designed to assist with daily living for the lower body. There are handy devices to help people who cannot use their lower limbs in abundance. These are hand-operated and provide independence to many disabled people. Simple things like calling for help are easily managed by people who can push a medical alarm button around the neck or make a telephone call. People can even drive cars with hand controls. But there were not many devices designed for people who had lost use of their upper body. Hand-operated devices were out of the question for Glen.

Glen did not want people to wait on him. In particular, he did not want outsiders waiting on him. One of the hardest things for him to do was accept help. Glen became determined to remain as self-reliant as possible. He began to work closely with Ronnie, to fashion all sorts of ingenious devices that enabled Glen to do things for himself and retain some of his independence.

He leaned forward to compensate for his lack of balance. He was still feeding himself for a while. He could use his hands a little bit, though he had little strength. He used tools from physical therapy and occupational therapy, the types of gadgets that stroke patients use to assist them to do simple tasks, like buttoning a shirt.

For a while, he could wear his jeans, but when that became impossible, he began to wear elastic-waist pants. It was a slow enough progression that adaption came gradually. Glen had difficulty turning doorknobs. So we changed the main entrance door with a new lever doorknob. Glen came up with the idea of a wooden lever and Ronnie helped to make them. These were fitted over other existing doorknobs. Using his forearm, Glen was able to open doors.

We installed a bidet for him, to allow him just that small amount of bathroom dignity. A bidet is a plumbing fixture similar to a toilet, either attached or adjacent to it, that enables hands-free cleansing of the genital area using spray water jets.

Glen made sure that the grandchildren stayed a little bit afraid of the bidet. Later on, they liked to get into his wheelchair, readjust his chair lift and program silly words and phrases into the mechanical talking machine he eventually acquired, but Glen didn't want them to play with the bidet.

Ronnie developed block-type devices for the bathroom to enable Glen to be able to use the toilet without assistance. One of the devices pulled his pants down; the other pulled them back up.

Glen had developed his own ways of using his body weight, and by maneuvering the parts of his body that he could still use, he managed to compensate and accomplish tasks that were no longer possible to do the conventional way.

Getting into and out of the car required some of that tricky maneuvering. Getting out was not as much a problem as getting in. Once, Glen leaned in the car too far, lost his balance and sort of bounced back out of the car. I don't know how he didn't get hurt. The next thing I knew he was lying on the grass laughing.

Little by little, every physical endeavor, however small, was becoming more of a challenge. One day, he wanted me to wire something at the houseboat, and I simply could not do it. He was frustrated with me, but I had to draw the line. I could not do it, no matter how much either of us wished I could.

Sometime after he was diagnosed, we went with family to the beach in Panama City, Florida. It was hot and Glen asked me to help him take off his shirt. Everyone gasped in shock. It was the first time they had seen the devastation of the disease, which had caused the muscles of his chest to atrophy. It upset him that they were upset. He wasn't vain, but it upset him that his appearance upset others. Eventually, he refused to look into a mirror, because he did not want to see his own face. He asked me, how can you stand to look at me? He did not realize that for a long time, no one looked at his face. Glen's appearance mattered to us only as an indicator of his illness, and we did not like what the illness was doing to him.

ZAC AND HIS BO, ON ONE OF OUR ANNUAL BEACH TRIPS.
LONG BEFORE ALS.

CHAPTER THIRTY-THREE

EMAILS

When the time came that he lost not only his strength and manual dexterity but also his ability to communicate, his world began to close in around him. He began to feel isolated. It broke his heart and to some extent his spirit. Depression settled in heavily. His interaction with people had always given him great joy. He cultivated his friendships with all people, old or young, rich or poor, fat or skinny, educated or not, pretty or ugly.

Now he couldn't speak and could no longer hold a pen to write. We began to fear that he might spend the remainder of his life confined to bed without the interaction with others that he so desperately needed. His spirits were so low that we all began to pray for him to find something to give purpose to his life. We had no idea what that might be.

Sometimes the stress of our plight became unendurable, the options so limited. When that happened, my brain whirled in circles and my thoughts became a tangled rats' nest.

One day, my daughter suggested that I call Ms Ruth. "You always do better when you talk to Ms Ruth." And she was right. Ms Ruth would help me to focus, and she would talk me through it.

"Ms Ruth" is Ruth Harrell, a veteran registered nurse of more than half a century. She is in her seventies and is now retired, although it seems that no one has told her that. She still actively lobbies in Washington on behalf of nurses. To watch her go about her daily schedule would exhaust most twenty-year-olds.

Ms Ruth is whip-smart, outspoken, warm, and thoroughly devoted to our family. She already knew me, but did not meet Glen until later.

"At the time that I met Glen, he had been diagnosed for a couple of years and was up and active and still able to speak, although his voice was going. I so well remember when our pastor would call on Glen to pray, everyone in the church would strain to hear him. He was such a tremendous man of faith," said Ruth Harrell.

She was as much help to Glen as she was to me. She often drove over just to sit with Glen and have a conversation. "We had such wonderful conversations," she says.

As Glen's voice became more and more difficult to understand, and he was becoming gradually more housebound, we all despaired.

Ms Ruth presented us with the solution. "I asked Glen what he thought about email."

That was all Glen needed to hear. He used his feet to type on a specially adapted keyboard. As poorly as Glen communicated by voice, he more than compensated with his emails. He sent comical ones, supportive words, and heartfelt messages.

Glen gave Ms Ruth permission to get email addresses from anyone at our church who wished to hear from him. We got sixty or seventy names at first and then when other people from outside the church heard about it they wanted to be added to the list. He sent Ms Ruth an email saying that all his modesty had gone by the wayside and told her I needed help. He was concerned about how much work I had to do.

His enthusiasm returned. He began a regular email newsletter. It helped him, and it helped our church to know how he was doing and to feel like they were contributing to his life. He found his purpose for yet another stage of life living with ALS.

I only discovered by accident how difficult it was for him to type those emails with his feet.

I needed to send a simple email from our home computer. As I started to do it, I realized his foot-operated keyboard was still attached. I was in a hurry and did not want to switch back to the standard keyboard.

I remember thinking: *how difficult can this be?*

If you want to know how difficult it can be, try typing something with your toes and you'll find out. It would have been much faster to simply switch the keyboards.

Over time, the disease became an invisible, unrelenting embezzler, stealing even the most basic of Glen's abilities to function as an able-bodied human. In time, the thief robbed him of his abilities to function without around-the-clock assistance.

CHAPTER THIRTY-FOUR

GLEN'S NEWSLETTER

Glen's new correspondence with emails solved one enormous problem and lifted his spirits tremendously. And that led him to write a newsletter.

MY THREE BATTLES

By Glen Maholovich

Hello to all my wonderful church friends.

I have gotten some great and loving feedback from some of you. Ever since my diagnosis, I have been asking God, "What is my purpose?"

I am going to take your feedback as a sign that for the moment, this is my purpose.

My goal is to share some of my life and get you to compare it with yours or someone you know. I realize some of my life may show the ugliness of the flesh, but I pray I can get you to see and believe that God is the only real source that you can depend on. My prayer for each of you is to have a close, personal intimate relationship with God, the Father, through Jesus Christ our Lord. You see, because of my weak commitment, it took 30 years before I committed to God the way He wanted me to in the first place. But that is another story.

This week I want to share with you my three greatest battles. Now the basics of these stories are true, but I may have stretched the truth a little on the details. I think you will know.

BATTLE NUMBER ONE

It was this past Christmas Eve. It had been a truly wonderful day. Vanessa was there, my children were there and my four wonderful grandchildren were there. We had such fun watching the grandchildren run and play. We had eaten a good meal, so everyone's belly was full. We had just finished opening gifts, so the grandchildren were running madly through the house. Even the adults were up, moving—all but me.

You see, this Christmas my darling daughter had decided to get her two children a little puppy dog. Now on the outside, she looks like a little angel. But on the inside, I think she may be a Demon Dog.

You see, the dog loves everyone, but me. I will be sitting in a chair minding my own business and here comes Demon Dog. She will sit there, stare up at me and bark. I am glad I don't speak "dog." Then when she has tormented me that way, she will jump all over me trying to bite me, I know. I think if she could jump high enough she would surely jump and sink her teeth in my throat. She wants blood.

Everyone is up moving around, and I know Demon Dog is hiding somewhere, waiting to attack me. Then, I remember one gift Vanessa had not opened. So I slowly get up and slowly move to the hall to ask Jacob about the present. Just then, Demon Dog sees only me. Being the cripple I am, Demon Dog knows she has me.

Like lightning, Demon Dog runs to my feet, grabs my right big toe and yanks with all her might. So here goes both of my feet across the floor with Demon Dog still pulling. I knew if she had not had a mouthful of toe, she would have hollered, "TIMBER!" So, I hit the floor with a loud thump. As I lay there on the floor, moaning and in pain, Demon Dog comes and plops up on my feet and smiled. That ordeal gave me an ambulance ride to the ER. Demon Dog and I are working on our relationship.

BATTLE NUMBER TWO

As we look at my second battle, I am found on the couch watching TV. Probably watching "NCIS." It is nighttime, Vanessa is in the office doing whatever she does in the office.

Like I said, I am on the couch minding my own business, when out of the corner of my eye; I spot him—a big ol' nasty roach.

Now, I dislike these things quite a lot. So, being the man of the house, I ease up off the couch—because the only way I can get up is slowly. Anyway, I am up and moving toward my target—just like (an agent of) "NCIS" would do.

When I reach that nasty roach, I try to put my foot down on top of him. Now if you didn't know, these big roaches, if you stomp on them, they will pop.

Anyway, this one did not pop, because I missed him.

Now it didn't take me long to figure out this was no ordinary roach. This was a NINJA ROACH. He began to run in and out of my feet, jumping, spinning—using all those many legs—showing his moves.

That is when I knew I was in trouble. Here was a cripple, trying to mash a NINJA ROACH (you know they show no mercy). He begins to jump, spin, kick and I don't know what else, he was moving so fast. And then, as he has worn me down, he ties my shoelaces together. With one mighty Ninja kick, there go my feet one way, and my body the other way.

Then came the familiar blame, pain and moaning. Vanessa came running in to find me once again on the floor.

Now she is such a dainty little thing she cannot pick me up. This time she calls my brother-in-law, Ronnie, to come pick me up.

It takes about 10 minutes for him to arrive.

During that time, I am laying on my right side, when some of the Ensure I had been fed decided to ooze out. Now here I am laying on the floor on my right side, in pain, moaning, with Ensure running out of my mouth, Vanessa getting something to clean me up.

Now I look over and see the NINJA ROACH doing a victory dance. All of a sudden, he sees the Ensure on the floor and licks his lips. But then Vanessa comes back. Now NINJA ROACH knows he is no match for the all-powerful "V."

You see, he has hurt her baby and she will go to the ends of the earth to protect her baby.

So Ronnie arrives. I am cleaned up and with their help; I am back on the couch telling them how much I had been mistreated by the NASTY NINJA ROACH.

Well, Ronnie looks around and spots mister nasty. Well, NINJA ROACH must figure, "I got myself another victim." Ronnie goes over to do battle, NINJA ROACH starts all of his spins, jumps, kicks, using all those legs, but after about three good stomps from Master Ronnie, NINJA ROACH was sent off to roach heaven. The only thing left for us to do was shout, and scrape him off the floor.

BATTLE NUMBER THREE

Now, I am sure you have heard the old saying: "Fact is stranger than Fiction." It is obvious I made up some of the first two battles, but this one is different. This one happened just the way I am going to tell it, and then you decide about strange facts.

It has been a day full of family. The kids and grandkids have been visiting. Now you never know what the day holds when they are all together. With their ages running from 12 down to almost two, the only thing you can count on is excitement.

Now every time I get a new gadget for my needs, they think they have gotten a new toy.

For example, I have a very expensive DynaVox machine I type words on, hit speak, and the machine speaks for me. Cool, huh? Well, all four of my grandchildren—bless their little hearts—they love to hit a whole line of letters just to see how the machine will pronounce it. The machine sits on a rolling cart.

Now, Keaton, almost two, loves to lay on the cart while he hits the letters and roll around. Bless his little heart.

Well, I got a Lift Assist Seat to help me get up off the couch. During this day, I had seen them on my seat, sometimes one, sometimes two. No big deal. Now I found out this little bit of info a little too late. The grandkids, bless their little hearts, were changing the tension on my Lift Seat trying to get it to catapult them into the air. Sounds fun, doesn't it?

Well, the day ends kids and grandkids leave and night falls. Vanessa is in the bedroom, exercising that already buff body. I am sitting on my Lift Assist Seat on the couch, probably watching "NCIS" on TV.

Now we have two couches. They are positioned in an L-shape, one on one wall, one on the other. Their ends almost touch.

I have a problem with my saliva glands running too much. That is one reason in church when I sometimes get choked, I cannot swallow all of the saliva that is produced. At home, that is not a big problem. I go to the bathroom and spit or I spit in a bucket I keep by the couch.

Now, do you remember my four grandchildren, bless their little hearts, had been at my home today?

So, there I am, sitting in my seat, which is on the left end of the couch. I might add, I was minding my own business, then my mouth fills up with saliva. No problem. I will spit into my bucket. Get this picture. My bucket in on the floor to my left side. I lean forward to my left to get over the bucket, as I have done many times before. I am almost there when my right cheek comes off the seat, just a little.

All of a sudden, the seat expands to full expansion. Next thing I know, I am up in the air headed to the floor, head first. Then comes the familiar thud of me hitting the floor, and the pain and of course, the moaning.

I am between the two couches, lying face down. I am on top of my spit bucket and the wires to my Dyna Vox machine. I can't move. All I can do is moan.

Vanessa, my dainty little wife, can't move me. She calls Jacob who hears me moaning over the phone. Suddenly Christmas Eve comes back into his memory. He—not knowing how badly I am hurt—makes it there in three minutes.

Thank God for Angels on Assignment. I am moaning when they pick me up, then all I can do is laugh. As you would know it, Vanessa gets mad at me because I think the fall is funny. After I filled them in on what happened, we all laughed, because they remembered all four of my grandchildren, bless their little hearts, being there and they knew exactly what had happened.

I trust you enjoyed my three battles. Do pray that I will not fall any more. I plan to write next about the 11 months after I was diagnosed. I am sorry, but there may not be any humor in that.

Thank you so much for letting me share.

In Christ's Love, I write

Glen Maholovich

PART FIVE

LEMONADE AND PUPPET SHOWS

Chapter thirty-five

NOW WHAT?

Glen was retired and we had finished whatever legal, financial and medical arrangements we were able to complete for the time being. We sold properties and stored things. We had moved to the river.

After that, we looked around and wondered what we were supposed to do next. How were we supposed to manage the next months — or years, please, God — of Glen's life? We had two options.

We could sit down, feel sorry for ourselves, hold our collective breath and live in a kind of holding pattern, waiting for Glen's demise. Or, we could make up our minds to fight back by living every moment we had for all we were worth.

All too often, the stance for living with a terminal illness is self-pity, anger, fear, bitterness, attention-seeking, despair, victim-hood and so on. Finding joy and purpose in the face of terminal, debilitating illness requires some effort, commitment, and creativity. The default position is easier, if vastly more miserable. Self-pity is a useless, miserable emotion that sucks the joy, the love and the life out of everyone it touches.

We wanted no part of it.

We reminded ourselves that this was the hand we'd been dealt. We hated it, we wished it were different, but we were powerless to change it. We did not intend to make what time together we had left count for nothing.

We opted for the latter. We fought back by aggressively seeking joy. So, we all shook our fists at the disease, and shouted to high heaven that we would not let it take one single thing more from us than we could help. And what we couldn't help it taking would not go without a fight.

We decided to create brand new memories, wonderful memories that we could call up years later when we needed to. We approached life with a renewed appreciation for every moment. The whole family committed to the new style of life. Every day would be a precious gift. Time is always precious, of course, but the constant awareness that life is gushing through the hourglass at double-time makes every single moment seem all the more priceless. Once it's gone, it's gone. We intended to live with all the gusto we could muster.

We chose to laugh. We cried together. We reminisced. We comforted one another and we held each other up. We made sure that we never left each other without saying, "I love you."

As far-fetched as it sounds, we succeeded, gloriously. We made memories. We experienced many moments of joy, bonding, affection and laughter. There were some moments of anger — mostly mine — and of course, some moments of melancholy.

There were more than a couple of instances of panic, some accompanied by ambulance rides. But there were many more moments of affection, tenderness, devotion and raucous hilarity. We did have to seek it, though. It wasn't going to come to us.

Glen showed us how to do that.

CHAPTER THIRTY-SIX

LEMONADE AND PUPPET SHOWS

We searched for ways that Glen could actively participate. I took a brief sabbatical in October of 2010 when Glen was still able to travel. We took a couple of short trips with friends, and we spent time together on our beloved houseboat enjoying nature and each other's company.

People who don't know any better sometimes shut sick people away. They probably mean well. But we did not want to do that. We wanted Glen to continue to be the husband, father, and active family participant in whatever way he could, for as long as he could. It turned out that he was able to do that in one way or another, almost until the day he died. Glen had great determination.

Glen went to every event with us. At first, when we went to ballgames he didn't want to sit in the bleachers, so he sat behind the outfield in a chair. People would go to him and talk to him. So soon, he found his way back to the bleachers. He could still walk for a long time. Later on, when he became weak, he still moved around the house in a sort of shuffle-gait. When he was very weak, we brought a chair for him to sit in, but he still went to the games.

Glen never willingly relinquished any parental or grand-parental activity that he could possibly accomplish. Glen learned to be a grandfather in his own way, using what he could. In many ways, able-bodied people could learn a thing or two from Glen.

The grandchildren may have been as good for his soul as any medicine could have been. Glen loved every single part of being a grandfather, the good, the poignant … and sometimes, the absurdly unexpected.

Years earlier, when Zac was much younger, he became fascinated by Glen's large big toe one day. All of us looked on as Zac marched over to where Glen's foot was exposed. We could see what Zac had in mind, but we all were so mesmerized that we could not bring ourselves to intervene. I suppose it was a little bit like watching a car crash and not quite believing what we were seeing. Zac stood over Glen's foot, bent over, took Glen's big toe in his mouth and chomped down. Glen naturally let out a whoop of surprise.

About a year after Glen was diagnosed, our daughter went into labor with her first child Ella. Glen wanted to be with his "baby" when she gave birth to her baby. But he was very weak, so he rested and slept on a hospital cot next to his daughter's bed.

When Ella hears anyone say that she was born during a dark year, she looks so hurt that we have to remind her that she was the one wonderful thing that happened that year.

When Ella was about a year or two old she got to where she would get away and run loose in the store, the way toddlers often do. Glen, our daughter and I were in a store and Ella got loose and started running all around. We had wandered away, leaving only Glen near Ella, when he saw her getting ready to run. Because Glen couldn't do anything at all with his upper body, he blocked her path with his legs.

Ella thought Glen was playing a game with her. She playfully poked her head through Glen's legs and he locked them down tight. At first, she thought it was fun. She was laughing. Then she realized that Glen was not going to let her go. That's when Ella got mad, and she made sure everyone within earshot knew about it.

Naturally, people in the store all glared disapprovingly at Glen, most likely wondering if they should intervene. But Glen stood his ground and held Ella in place until we got there.

One day I asked Glen what he would do first if he could have his strength back. Without taking even a second to consider it, he said, "I would pick up and hold Ella." Glen had never been able to pick her up as he had the other grandchildren. She could be placed in his lap supported by pillows, but he could not lift her. It broke his heart.

Glen performed puppet shows for the grandchildren. With appropriately decorated socks on his feet, he performed the action and they made up stories.

When our friends Keith and Debbie Lisenby found out that Glen performed tootsie-powered puppet shows for his grandchildren, they talked him into performing one for them. We took a trip together with them and some other friends, Dudley and Sheila Fountain. During that trip, Glen performed a puppet show that he had written. I read from the script while he performed it. There was a male sock puppet and a female sock puppet.

Glen had the G-rated version of the puppet show for the family and the children, but he wrote one slightly more adult for Keith, Debbie, Dudley and Sheila. It was adult, not crude, and naturally, because Glen wrote it, it was humorous.

We all wanted and needed him to be a part of the family, not an onlooker. We sought out activities he could do with us. We found some Wii video games that he could operate with his feet. We had a terrific time playing them.

One of our favorite things to do as a family was to make freshly squeezed lemonade. We used my mother's old lemon squeezer and the grandchildren helped. They loved the process of making the lemonade just as much as drinking the finished product.

The grandchildren, themselves, devised a plan for Glen to be a part of that process. As anyone who has ever tried to squeeze juice from a lemon knows, the first step is to roll the lemon on a hard surface to break up the citrus membranes to release the juices. One day the children decided that the job of lemon rolling would be perfect for Glen. He could still move his feet, so that he could roll the lemons on the floor to release the juice. One lemon at a time, these small children carried lemons to their grandfather. They stood by as he rolled each one on the floor and then proudly carried them back to me for cutting and juicing. Whenever a lemon would slip from under Glen's foot and roll away, they ran to chase it down, giggling all the way, causing Glen's eyes to light up.

ELLA'S 5TH BIRTHDAY. ONE YEAR BEFORE GLEN'S DEATH

CHAPTER THIRTY-SEVEN

SNOWTUBING

Glen still loved the outdoors, so we took him out wherever we went — ball games, recitals, family events, meals out, road trips, everything. One year we traveled across the Alabama-Tennessee line to find a certain train that would go up a mountain so we could see the pretty fall foliage.

We got on the train and went up the mountain. Glen was not impressed. He just looked at us as if to say, "You drove all this way for this?"

During the Christmas season of 2008, we decided that our family gift to one another would be a vacation in a place that would feel like the Christmas depicted in holiday cards. We wanted to feel all the elements of Christmas where it was cold. Christmas time in southern Alabama can sometimes be balmy enough to wear shorts. Since snow is a rare occurrence, we decided to head out and find some.

The plan was to do absolutely nothing but relax as a family. We rented a cabin in South Carolina. Our family, including grandchildren, were present. We ate meals together, we played games, we went snow tubing and some even tried skiing.

We were determined to be festive, which for us isn't all that difficult. We have always known how to have fun together. Glen's upper body was paralyzed, but he was still moderately ambulatory.

Glen had always been the athlete in the family. I was not. But for whatever reason I found that I excelled at snow tubing. I zipped down the slope, basking in my speed. It was great fun.

I was proud of myself. I was winning races down the slope. Winning races, for a non-athlete, is a terrific ego boost. I was having the time of my life.

During one particular run, Glen was tubing toward the end of the track, just ahead of me. Glen's strength and energy, already limited, had somewhat depleted from the physical exertion of climbing. He did not have the ability to maneuver his body in order to stop his tube at the end of the track. We chose a "spotter," to stand at the end of track to stop Glen and help him out of the tube. The spotter was standing at the bottom to do that, but in this case, he was also filming us.

I was bearing down fast.

At that moment, however, the spotter was trying to focus the camera. He knew that Ella and Keaton would be coming down next. He was looking down at the camera and didn't realize that Glen was directly in my path as I was zooming down the slope. He was frantically trying to get out of my way.

Glen saw me before I could realize how close I was. He had learned to manipulate his body so that he could kind of rock his body to get up. He was doing that when he saw me.

He struggled to rise up and fling himself out of the tube to avoid the pummeling I was about to inflict. After that, he tried to roll himself out of the tube. Glen simply did not have the strength to get all the way out.

The spotter, however, was unaware of any of this, as he was still trying to adjust his camera.

Glen stared at me with panicked, wide-open eyes. He knew he could not escape.

Finally, the spotter looked up — just in time to see me slam into Glen at top speed. Glen went spinning around. Then he tumbled out. He was unhurt, but his masculine pride had to be deeply wounded But then he laughed. Because he was Glen. We all started laughing.

Glen did not tube anymore. From then on, he waited at the finish line for the rest of us, cheering us on. But he took great pains to stand clear of me when I was the one coming his way.

Chapter thirty-eight

BATHROOM BREAKS

We traveled several times with Bruce and Susan Lovett, the friends we met through Building Hope. We discovered that even though we had not known each other long, we became fast friends.

By this time, Glen was no longer able to eat by mouth, which caused Bruce, among others, to feel uncomfortable. "You are taught your whole life that it is impolite to eat in front of someone who is not eating. We were uncomfortable eating in front of Glen, but he did not want us to feel bad. He insisted that we go ahead. He loved socializing with friends and even when he couldn't eat, he wanted to be present. One time I ordered a rib eye, which is one thing I know he loved and could not eat. And he just smiled."

On certain trips, Bruce remembers some particularly awkward, but funny, situations regarding misunderstandings by strangers. They were the sort of experiences that are uncomfortable at the time, but funny later.

Bruce told the story of one unusual bathroom visit. "We were in a steak house one time, and Glen had to go to the bathroom. Of course, he couldn't go by himself, so Vanessa needed to go in with him to help him. We checked to make sure that no one else was in the men's room and then she went in with Glen. I stood at the door to stand watch and make sure no one else went in.

"As they were inside, a gentleman tried to go in, but I stopped him, I told him he could not go in because there was a man in there with his wife. Well he looked at me real funny. Then he stalked off to get the manager. The manager came over and said, 'I want to know just what's going on in there.'

"After I explained the situation to him, he understood and told us to carry on."

After that, it seemed prudent for Bruce to be the one to go in with Glen. That prompted a different misinterpretation by onlookers. On another restaurant outing, Bruce went in to help Glen with his pants. By this time, Glen wore only elastic-waist pants and slip-on shoes.

"We went into a stall to do that. There were other men in the restroom, and I don't know what they were thinking when Glen and I both came out of the same stall . . . but we got some looks," Bruce said.

That was an exercise in compassion and humility for both of them. He certainly did not enjoy having another man, a friend, take down his pants for him, and then take them back up.

"Glen was so gracious and humble," Bruce said. "I would never have gone into a bathroom stall to help another man. I joked with Glen, 'You know I have to care a lot about you to do this.' And the truth is I did. Glen was a very special person. He was an exceptional person. Glen dealt with the indignities of his illness far better than I might have."

CHAPTER THIRTY-NINE

HILLBILLY CHICKS

Another misinterpretation that occurred, again at a restaurant and this time at a little café, happened after Susan and I had left the table to go to the bathroom.

According to Bruce this is what happened:

"Well, these two hillbilly women — I mean they were actually hillbilly women — struck up a conversation with Glen and me, and the next thing we knew they were inviting us to go to their house. I might point out here that the two ladies were dressed considerably more provocatively than typical country ladies," Bruce said.

A few minutes went by and Susan and I came out of the restroom. We looked at our husbands and we immediately realized what was going on. We were amused, so we decided to sit down at another table to watch. Bruce and Glen knew we were there, but the flirtatious hillbilly women had no idea we were their wives.

We watched Bruce and Glen squirming under our gaze.

"We were close to closing the deal, but we never quite got there," Bruce joked.

Finally, we made our presence known and the hillbilly vixens backed off.

Sibling photo, Mary Ann, Glen, Brenda

CHAPTER FORTY

JOYRIDES

Our relationship wasn't all lollipops, rosebuds and candy kisses. There were times when even Glen's tragic, vulnerable plight did not shield him from my temper — especially when he did something especially risky. He still drove a car for a longer time than he should have. Glen drove by pressing his forearms against the steering wheel. It was becoming scary. Glen drove me back from Pensacola to Atmore after a medical procedure. I was medicated, so I could not drive. It was a nerve-wracking hour, during which we both realized that his driving days were at an end. That was about the middle of 2009.

When I said I was afraid he would get in an accident, he joked darkly about that.

"It would be just my luck," he said, "that even if I tried to throw myself in front of a car, he would run over me, but I would survive."

It was only after I pointed out that someone else might be hurt that he agreed to stop driving; one more blow to his independence and pride.

There was a time when our builder friend, Keith Lisenby, was driving us all to the river. It was during our first move to the houseboat and he was helping us to move some things into it.

I warned him ahead of time that Glen would tell him precisely how to drive every inch of the way. And sure enough, that's exactly what he did.

Glen kept telling Keith he was doing it wrong. I kept telling Glen that Keith had been driving many years and he knew what he was doing.

But Keith didn't mind. Just as Keith had understood when Glen critiqued his home-building techniques, he understood that Glen's driving instructions were his way of retaining a tiny shred of self-respect and pride.

"When there is so much you can no longer do, that you used to do, and there are so many things happening to you that you cannot control, you have to find something that you feel like you have some control over," Keith said.

Well, even if Keith understood, there were times when I had all of Glen's critiquing that I could take. One time, when he was again telling me how to drive and we were not that far from home, I booted him out of the car. Not literally, of course, but I was annoyed and I stopped the car.

I told him to get out.

"Okay, Glen! You don't like the way I'm driving. Well then, you can just walk. You can still do that." But the angriest I ever got at Glen occurred during our second occupancy of the houseboat.

Glen's symptoms had advanced to the point that I worried about him when he was at the houseboat alone. I had a thirty or forty minute drive to work. The necklace monitor buttons that are so popular with people who are injured in a fall and cannot get up were not an option for him. He could not use his hands or fingers to push the buttons. I was afraid that something would happen while he was alone.

Glen had already made it clear that he did not want to be babied or taken care of like a child, but my fear for his safety trumped that. We compromised. I would call him every day at lunch and check on him.

That worked out okay, until the day I called him and he did not answer. *Well,* I thought, *that could happen.* I waited a minute and called him again. No answer. I called again. Still no answer. I did not know what was wrong, but I knew for sure that it couldn't be anything good. I told my coworkers that something was wrong at home and I had to leave. I grabbed my keys and took off for the houseboat.

When I finally arrived, my fears intensified. He was not there. Not anywhere. I looked all over. I started checking with the neighbors and not one of them had seen him. That lingering fear I had of him falling into the water and drowning began to overwhelm me.

Before long, the neighbors joined the search for Glen. I began to notice that the neighbors were surreptitiously glancing off the edge of the deck, toward the water. They, too, were worried that he might have fallen in.

Just about the time I was sick inside at the certain knowledge that he had fallen into the water, I glanced down the road and saw a truck slowly driving toward us. The people in the truck seemed to be on a leisurely afternoon sightseeing tour.

I recognized the truck and the driver. It was our friend Richard Keesler. Then I recognized the happy-go-lucky passenger. It was Glen, smiling and looking around as though he hadn't a care in the world.

I lost it. I was livid. I was so furious I was shaking from head to toe.

Glen must have seen the look on my face because he suddenly stopped smiling.

One of our river-road neighbors who had been part of the search party leaned over, half-smiling, and whispered to me, "I hope you take him in the house and wear him out over this."

I headed for the truck, jerked open the door and let him know exactly how I felt about his impromptu joyride.

"Don't ever do that again!" I told him how terrified I was that he had fallen over and drowned. His casually morbid answer to that did not make me feel any better.

"So? What if I had?" Glen responded. "What a way to go."

Even in jest, Glen's casual quips about death chilled me.

My sister, Jennifer, asked me once if I thought Glen was suicidal. I can say positively that he was not. That was not in his nature. Despite his occasional use of dark humor, we all knew as surely as we knew anything that Glen wanted to live as long as he possibly could. He fought for every second of his life and we all knew that.

"The only reason I don't want to die is that I don't want to leave you and the kids, but I am in a win-win," he said. "If I die, I go to heaven, if I don't I get to stay with you," Glen said, again and again.

CHAPTER FORTY-ONE

TRAIN STATION

Most of the time when Glen talked at all about his own death, he spoke of it as that journey aboard the passenger train to heaven. He talked about people he loved who had boarded the train before he did. He talked about how happy he would be to see them again. He explained in his patient way that his own car was scheduled to arrive at the Station earlier than other cars. He said he knew we'd all be along when it was our time. He said he would be waiting at the terminal for each arrival. He said repeatedly, "Make sure they all come. I'll be waiting."

He was adamant that each person be aboard that train so that he could see them again.

Even after his diagnosis and when a second opinion confirmed it, for a long time we stood resolute in our belief that he would be healed. That may seem naïve, but we had our reasons for believing that and we had faith.

At some point, I had acquired an article published by a Christian organization about a woman diagnosed with ALS who was healed through prayer. I knew that if God would do that for her, he certainly could do it for Glen. If anyone deserved healing, it was Glen. We counted on that.

I pleaded with God in my journal:

"I am so tired. I feel as if I am sinking deeper under the load. Please hurry and come to my rescue! I'm losing my husband, my life, as I know it and I don't like it! When does all of this come to an end? When?"

March 19, 2010

CHAPTER FORTY-TWO

TOBY AND MAGGIE

G len had given ALS support groups a shot, but discovered that they depressed him too much to be of any benefit. Knowing that there would be no remission for him, watching and interacting with patients in later stages provided no comfort. They served only to remind him of his own grim future.

But he did form a strong bond with Toby Quimby, a man he knew in Atmore, whose symptoms and experience with being diagnosed were eerily similar to Glen's.

Toby's symptoms began about two years after Glen's.

Toby and Maggie Quimby lived in our town, and Toby and Glen had known of each other for years. The Quimbys were about ten years younger than we were, with three energetic young boys at home, which is why our social circles had not intersected.

Toby managed a funeral home in town. He was well known in the community, just as Glen was from his work at the bank.

It was uncanny how similar our two families' experiences had been. Toby had experienced pain with his illness, which Glen had not, but many of their other symptoms, coupled with the initial diagnostic quest, were so similar.

Over a couple of years and numerous visits to various specialists, Toby had finally learned he had Lyme's Disease with complications. It eventually became a serious autoimmune disease. At one point, Toby spent nearly eight months in Missouri to receive intravenous treatments twice a day. For quite a long time, it seemed that Toby would not survive. Fortunately, however, he has since stabilized. Toby is still very ill, but he is better.

We all became close friends when the husbands were ill. We started to go out to dinner together. "We used to watch Glen go get huge bowls of ice cream. He loved ice cream. He really loved ice cream. Ice cream was one of the remaining foods he could still eat, and he made the most of that," Toby said.

I remember when we first got to know each other, I felt so sad for them that they still had young children at home while they were dealing with this difficult illness. The day Glen was diagnosed I remember thanking God that our children were grown. I watched Maggie juggle working her job, taking care of her children, shuttling them to school events and taking care of Toby, all at the same time. I was so amazed that she could do it. Maggie said she was amazed by what I could do.

Extreme, constant fatigue was common for each man. Toby could not even do the daily things he used to do, Maggie said. He had been the manager of the funeral home for years, but was then physically unable to go to work. She said it took all of his energy for Toby to get a simple shower. As soon as he was finished, he had to go back and lie down. He would sleep and sleep and sleep. It was the same way with Glen.

Just as each of the men had been forced to adapt to their physical ailments, so had the two of us. I had learned to decipher Glen's meaning when he spoke and others could not understand.

Maggie and I could empathize when others would have trouble understanding. We both understood the exhaustion, the emotional roller coaster, the juggling of so many plates in the air and tendency for hyper-vigilance. We became mutual supports for one another. We worried about our husbands and our husbands worried about us.

Maggie was struck by the love we still felt for each other.

"You see many great couples, but Glen and Vanessa were different," Maggie said. "They were truly, truly in love. You could tell, by the way their eyes lit up. Every time we were around them, and she spoke to Glen, she lit up. I never, ever heard her complain. And there are times when, even though you love your husband, you get so very tired. Vanessa was so totally focused on helping her man, and that inspired me to be that way for Toby."

As ill as Toby was, he said he had great difficulty watching Glen get sicker and sicker. When we all first became friends, Glen was still able to walk and participate in things, but Toby watched sadly as his friend's health declined.

"We would go down to their boathouse and visit on the deck, and he would walk slowly, his upper body was weak, and he would become extremely tired. That was so hard for us to watch," Toby said.

But like Maggie and me, Toby and Glen could commiserate.

"Only another person who is experiencing a debilitating illness can truly understand what it is like and to talk to another person who does understand is a relief," Toby said.

At the same time, both men were equally concerned about burdening the other. "Glen did not want anyone to ever pity him. He wanted to make people around him feel better," Toby said. In an email, Glen wrote about that:

Toby, my friend.

I trust you are doing well. We have talked before and you don't seem to have the mental struggles that I have. I thank God for that. We have been in this battle for over eight years and I pray I do not depress you. And if you had rather I not share any of my feelings, please let me know, you will not offend me at all. So many of us have so many different symptoms and of course, we handle it differently.

"We never really talked about dying, but I would talk about what I was going through, and Glen would talk about what he was going through," Toby said. "As he grew so much weaker, Glen might occasionally speak to me of friends or family he looked forward to seeing in Heaven. Glen would turn something others saw as negative into something beautiful.

"He was so very ill, but he always thought about the other person. He wanted to make people around him feel better," Toby said. He nearly always succeeded. Toby admired the strength of Glen's faith and hoped that he would be so strong in his own final days.

"The thing is, that people in this situation tend to go one of two ways," Toby said. "Either they grow closer to God or they grow farther away.

Glen grew close. Some people want to blame God. Sometimes people who never believed in God before will still blame God."

Maggie said, "The Glen that we knew was just grateful to be alive one more day. He was extremely grateful to God and he wanted to show everyone around him that he was grateful. I think that I will always remember that. When it comes time for me to die, I hope that I can show the courage and grace that Glen showed."

Glen was not a bit worried about dying, Maggie remembered. "He knew where he was going. He was only worried about Vanessa, and his children, and his grandchildren, and of course his friends. It was clear to me that he was positive he was going to Heaven."

Both of them think Glen would be proud of me now. I am not so sure. I am better than I was. And I have learned to live my life on my own, in practical terms. But I miss Glen. After Glen died, Toby took me by the hand and gently walked with me to say my final goodbye to my husband.

PART SIX
CAREGIVING

CHAPTER FORTY-THREE

UNPREPARED

Glen's illness propelled me into the world of caretaking, which I thought I understood. My understanding didn't come close to reality. My previous view of caretaking — probably many people's view — was similar to the view a babysitter has of parenting compared with the view of a full-time parent. I had an abstract, professional idea that life for a caregiver is difficult.

As a nurse, I had more experience with the subject than the average person. I had been in and out of homes where I assisted other family caregivers. After I became a caretaker myself, I discovered all those visits provided me with just a peek through the blinds of a caretaker's world. I had never considered it something I would do.

Until you walk in a caregiver's shoes, you can only imagine the overwhelming burden. Caregiving is the hardest, most relentlessly labor-intensive endeavor you can imagine. It is physically demanding, but worse, it is emotionally overwhelming. The round-the-clock demands of caregiving often lead to burnout.

Whatever needs a caregiver has, take a back seat to the insistent demands of the disease. If the caregiver has children at home or a full-time job or any other obligations, the caregiver's needs wind up all the way back in the trunk of the car, underneath the old clothes you keep meaning to donate to charity.

Before his illness, I had my own interests; Glen had his own interests; and we had shared interests. Our lives were well balanced and we were both happy. After his illness, and especially during the last year, the disease dictated my life, just as it did his.

Burnout is a real condition and it is paralyzing. Life becomes a desperate effort to exist from one moment to the next.

My usual source of support and physical assistance had enough on his mind. Glen's own plate was spilling over. Glen had to come to terms with his own losses. He struggled to adapt to the disabling symptoms of his disease. We each went through the day with mountains on our backs.

I suffered another unexpected blow during that time. My mother died suddenly in her sleep.

When she didn't come to the door one day, Glen broke into the house, where we found she had passed away. We found out later that she had lung cancer, a fact she herself had not learned. It may have been God's blessing that she died so gently and quietly in her sleep. I could never have watched these two people I loved so much simultaneously suffer prolonged misery followed by death. I surely would have lost my mind.

When my mother died, I could not shed tears. I was distraught, but the tears would not come. The antidepressants I was taking dulled the intensity of my emotions. More than that, however, I had learned to compartmentalize my brain so that I could push away distractions, emotions — any thought but that of the immediate task — off into a corner somewhere. It was essential for me to tune out whatever emotion or information was not necessary to the moment at hand, or my brain could not have handled the overload.

Glen's physical health care slowly took over my life. I began to feel as if I were outside my own body, hovering, watching myself move robotically through each task. I had neither the energy nor time to indulge my own heartbreak. The grief I felt for the loss of my mother, the loss of my old life, my husband's plight, the loss of my time, of my identity, had to be shoved to the side. Grief would have to wait.

So much of that period remains a blur to me, like a dream, snippets of which I remember in a hazy fog.

My family was concerned.

"I was much more worried about Mom than I was about Daddy," Jacob said. "I honestly believed that she would have a nervous breakdown. She was almost robotic. She was on autopilot. She was hyper-vigilant, standing watch, standing guard," he said. "Daddy was worried about Mom, too."

Chapter forty-four

CAREGIVER
STRESS SYNDROME

The large number of unpaid caregivers has gone unrecognized for the most part. However, one category of caregivers has received federal recognition. The Caregivers and Veterans Omnibus Health Services Act of 2010 recognizes the value of family members who care for combat wounded and disabled veterans. The act established a program of assistance for their unpaid caregivers as well as veterans, with benefits covering counseling and mental health services under the Department of Veterans Affairs.

"Caregiver Stress Syndrome," which is not in the "Diagnostic and Statistical Manual of Mental Disorders," is widely known within the medical community. The syndrome afflicts some sixty-six million Americans, who act as unpaid caregivers for family members who require special round-the-clock assistance at home for many months or years. Caregiver stress is serious and incapacitating. Symptoms include prolonged depression, anxiety and insomnia, feelings of inadequacy and guilt and feeling overwhelmed, frustrated, and angry. The condition frequently leads to physical problems, partly from the strain and partly because, in looking after the primary patient, caregivers neglect their own health.

Unpaid caregivers include parents of seriously ill or disabled children, adult children of Alzheimer patients, spouses of combat-injured veterans and adult children of frail, elderly parents, among many others.

Burnout is real. Caregiver Stress Syndrome is real. It is debilitating and it is miserable. I experienced it. Often Glen would tell us not to live our lives around his disease, but that wasn't easy to do. The disease called the shots.

We had a schedule. Each day I came home from work. I fed Glen, bathed him, shaved him, and turned him. I positioned him to be comfortable. I helped him sit down and I helped him get back up. Physically, it was like caring for a nearly 200-pound newborn.

Day after day, I found myself dashing breathlessly from one spinning plate atop a pole to another spinning plate, then another, zipping back and forth, exhausting my energy and stealing what I could from the next day to keep my plates from crashing to the ground. There was no downtime. No rest.

It has been so long since I have made an entry. I have been so overcome with the burden of Glen's illness that I haven't the energy or strength to write down my thoughts. It seems all my energy has been taken to just get through each day. Good things have happened, but Glen's situation weighted me down. It is so hard to continue with daily life when you have to watch someone you love suffer.

Thankfully, he doesn't have physical pain but watching him lose his abilities to even complete his activities for daily living is overwhelming. The hardest is to see my strong, self-sufficient husband of more than 200 pounds lose down to 166 pounds. He is so tired and fatigued he can barely move from the bed to the couch."

— Journal, February 20, 2010

Glen urged me to do the ordinary things I found enjoyable, and I tried my best. I had my nails manicured, had lunch with friends, went shopping, did exercises and read books I enjoyed. Maybe it sounds frivolous to do such things when my husband was imprisoned by his own body at home. But my sanity was at serious risk. If I lost my sanity, I would not have been able to care for Glen.

Those occasional hours outside the house with a girlfriend were critical, even if there were too few of them. Still, to do those simple things required time-consuming and complicated arrangements. Someone had to stay with Glen. Even going to church on a Sunday required a friend to stay back with him. I was fortunate. I had wonderful family and friends who volunteered to stay with Glen. I should have accepted outside help sooner than I did, but I had trouble turning Glen's care over to others.

CHAPTER FORTY-FIVE

JACOB

Jacob moved in with us following his tour in Iraq. It was a blessing for all of us, even in ways we didn't expect. We knew that he would be able to help in very practical ways. He was strong and could do things I couldn't, and he was one more pair of eyes and ears.

We hadn't anticipated the psychological wonder drug the grandchildren would be for Glen. They stayed with us on weekends. Glen began to live for weekends. His face lit up with joy when they were with us.

Jacob found helping his father to be something natural, something he did without a second thought. We soon discovered what a great difference there is between helping others and receiving help from others. One is easy. The other is not.

Glen resisted help for himself, but he had no problem at all providing help to his aging father without batting an eye.

Jacob said, "Daddy never complained, and he never tried to push Paw-Paw off to some nursing home," Jacob said. "I didn't even think about it much at the time. But I remember that once Paw-Paw had an accident in his clothes, and Daddy went in and he took his clothes off and he cleaned him up and showered him. He just did it, without complaining, even though he probably didn't really enjoy it. Later on, when Daddy got sick, and I had to do that for him, I thought back to that. Nobody particularly likes doing those things, but they have to be done."

CHAPTER FORTY-SIX

GLEN'S RESISTANCE TO HELP

I t's one thing to need help and even to know that you need help, but it's an entirely different thing to be comfortable with accepting that help.

In my work as a nurse, I saw people resist help all the time.

I don't think I understood the powerful hold such resistance takes until I experienced a need for help myself. Accepting help is humbling. It brings with it a sense of vulnerability, of feeling indebted to or beholden to others. Those are uncomfortable feelings. It didn't matter that our family and friends assured us they truly wished to help. We knew they were sincere. We weren't martyrs. But there may have been a thought in the back of our minds that if we accepted help we were somehow neglecting our responsibility.

Both Glen and I resisted help. But my discomfort with accepting help paled against Glen's. He was so uncomfortable that he kept the level of his difficulties secret from me. He didn't want me to know how much help he needed.

My heart broke the first time I went to his office and saw how far behind he was with his paperwork and realized that he had not touched anything at all for months. That was so unlike him. He had always been compulsive about business paperwork.

I had to start watching him closely to learn the full extent of his impairments. Despite the fact that his deteriorating health more and more required it, Glen still hated to have anyone wait on him. For Glen it meant surrendering a little bit more of his adult independence. I always considered his wishes, although he usually wanted more independence than was safe for him. We got into some heated arguments over his stubbornness. He drove a car much longer than he should have. He continued to go out in a boat with only our grandson Zac aboard because he wanted to teach Zac how to navigate a river as he had taught Jacob. Glen stayed alone at home much longer than was safe for him. He had begun to fall, which for him was extremely dangerous.

Twice he ended up in the emergency room. Falls were particularly difficult for him. First, because he did not have strength or the use of his hands and arms to get himself back up, and second, because of his size and weight I could not get him up by myself. Sometimes it took two, sometimes three people to get him back up.

He fell one time on Christmas Eve. It was a tradition that he always got me chocolate-covered cherries at Christmas time, and he entrusted that to someone else this year. He had gone back to check on them when he tripped over the grandchildren's new puppy.

Keaton had just begun to toddle and he was right under Glen as he began to fall. Glen knew he couldn't stop the fall, so he contorted his body to avoid falling on Keaton.

Keaton was screaming. There was a huge crash. I still remember the faces of the grandchildren as the ambulance picked him up. I rode in the ambulance with him to translate.

Glen minimized the falls. He refused to acknowledge how serious they were. He made jokes, even when we knew he had to be in pain and he must have been frightened. He may have wished to spare those around him, but we worried anyway.

I know now that resisting help in such circumstances makes as much sense as driving a car with your emergency brake engaged. There's no good reason for it. It doesn't help and it can even be a detriment.

That applies to both the patient and the family caregivers.

Maggie, who felt all the same vulnerabilities accepting help, remembered how hard it was for her, too. "You don't realize how much pride you have until something like this happens and then you have to humble yourself."

She stressed that support is essential.

"You cannot handle this without a very strong support system of friends and family. It's crucial to stay close to your church family, and let them know what is going on and let them help you. If you're not in a church family, try to find one. But if you do not have or cannot find a church family, you need to find some network of support. You can draw on your actual family members or your friends from work or clubs. There are organizations that can point you to support groups and professional assistance. The important thing, the thing that is hard for most people, is to accept help early. Don't put it off out of pride," Maggie said.

In hindsight, I would give exactly that same advice.

CHAPTER FORTY-SEVEN

NORMALCY AT WORK

My job had become my last refuge. It was a place where I could go and focus on other people and other things. I could think about something besides my own circumstances. It enabled me to retain some sanity. It was the only thing normal in my life. At work, I could focus on other people and do other things. For a brief while, I did not obsess about my husband dying slowly at our home. My job kept me from social isolation. When I left work for the weekend, I would more than likely not leave my house until Monday morning when it was time to return to work.

Even though as a nurse I was a caregiver of sorts, it was not the same as caregiving for my husband. At work, I could, and needed to, remain emotionally detached and objective. If I had not had those other things to occupy my mind, I would have gone crazy. I was on a tight schedule, which did not include time for grief or for going crazy.

CHAPTER FORTY-EIGHT

BREAKING POINT

When Glen was still eating by mouth but only with great difficulty, he began losing weight at an alarming pace. This was dangerous. Already we had been forced to limit his diet because so many foods caused horrible choking. We needed to find an alternate way for him to receive the nutrients he needed.

He needed to have a PEG tube inserted. PEG stands for percutaneous endoscopic gastrostomy. A tube, accessible from outside the abdomen, is inserted into the patient's stomach through the abdominal wall. After the feeding tube is inserted, patients can still eat orally, so long as they can safely chew and swallow.

The decision to have the PEG placement was difficult. It was the admission of the beginning of the end. But he lost nine pounds in less than two weeks. It was the PEG tube or starvation.

A day after his 53rd birthday the PEG was placed. We both had a peace about it. What a difference. He is now talking and laughing. The Lord surely answered my prayer and gave me my husband back. Life is short. There is no promise of tomorrow. I pray we live each day to the fullest.

—Journal, February 15, 2010

Glen's foods consisted of baby food and the supplement drink, Ensure, blended, loaded into a syringe and pushed through his peg. The grandchildren sometimes tried to feed him his favorite foods through the PEG tube, even though they knew and he knew that he would not be able to taste them. He played along.

CHAPTER FORTY-NINE

TEAM MAHOLOVICH

My exhaustion was at odds with Glen's resistance. We reached an impasse. It became an emotional tug-of-war. Glen's insistence on independence pulled hard against my fears for his safety. His insistence that I be the primary person to help him smashed up against my perpetual state of near-collapse.

We reached a sort of compromise.

He began to allow family members to help, to a degree. Team Maholovich sprang into action.

Jacob helped me to take care of Glen throughout the night. Sometimes close friends would stay over one night during the week. Each of us had our regular responsibilities, our jobs and school. Some family members had to come in from out of town. We all did whatever we could when we could carve out time. Family members stayed with us on weekends. Including Glen's sisters and his brother-in-law, Ronnie.

Our friend Susan Lovett was struck by the courage and strength of our family as a whole. "In my entire experience, I don't think I have ever seen a family so supportive of someone's dignity," Susan said. "They were so supportive of him and allowed him to make his own decisions and maintain as much of his dignity as possible. Glen was courageous, but so were they."

Whitney, Jacob's finance at the time, was struck by Glen's humility and gracious acceptance of his illness. "I deal with people all the time who complain about how bad their lives are," Whitney said. "And they really don't have anything to complain about. I saw Glen, who couldn't speak and couldn't hold his head up, still caring about everybody else and making other people laugh," Whitney said. "He was always mainly interested in everyone else. That just showed me that some people have it so much worse, without complaining at all."

"Even when he was very ill, Glen did not focus on himself," Whitney said. He wanted to know how she was doing and what was going in her life.

"Glen would ask me, 'Did you arrest anyone today?'" Whitney said.

He was fascinated with the crime shows on television during that time, like "Criminal Minds," "NCIS," and "Bones" and all those. Jacob was off taking classes to finish his degree, so Glen and Whitney developed a twice-weekly standing date to watch those shows together on television. Every Tuesday and Thursday night when those programs aired, Whitney dropped by and the two of them watched show after show after show.

Glen apologized to Jacob and Whitney for "messing up date nights" by spending their time with him. But Whitney never saw it that way. "You know a lot of people think that going through this with him, watching him, knowing him at his most vulnerable and at his sickest, would be a really awful thing, but I think of it as a blessing. I did hate seeing him go through this, of course, but watching him taught me so much."

Glen used his big toe to operate the television remote. "Sometimes when people in the house were talking too loud or making too much noise while he was watching the shows, he used his big toe to turn up the remote as loud as it could go, which was his signal for people to be quiet so he could hear his show."

CHAPTER FIFTY

GLEN FEARS ABANDONMENT

Glen in his helplessness watched me and worried about me. He knew what a toll it was taking. One day I noticed Glen sitting on the couch with a troubled look on his face. I asked him what was wrong, thinking he was downhearted by the progression of the disease.

I was surprised when his eyes filled with tears. He told me about an email he had received from a fellow ALS patient he knew. The other patient wrote Glen that his wife had left him and had taken their child. She told the stricken man that it was all too much for her, that the stress of being a caregiver was more than she could handle. I knew at once that Glen was fearing the same fate. I looked at my husband with tears in his eyes.

Glen was well aware of the extent of care he required. He became apologetic. He referred to himself as a burden. "You must really love me to do all this," he said.

That was exactly the reason I was doing it, and I told him so. I reminded him that if the situation were reversed, he would be caring for me in the same way. Then I reminded him that he had not chosen to be ill, nor had he carelessly done something to risk becoming ill. I knew he would have done anything he could have to have prevented it, I told him. I assured him that I would never abandon him, and neither would his family and friends.

That does not mean I condemn the woman who fled from the awfulness of the disease. I am ashamed to admit that there were times that I, too, wanted to flee, to run away. The crushing weight of responsibility for his care at times became unendurable. Loved ones fold under the strain and run away more often than most people realize.

I understand how that woman probably felt, and I can hardly judge anyone whose strength simply cannot hold out. It could just as easily have been me.

I am a strong person, with a strong faith in God. I'm an experienced nurse and I have a wonderful support system and loving family who live nearby, yet there were times that I felt that I would surely buckle under the strain. I was extremely fortunate.

I do not know the woman's circumstances. I do know she had a child. The woman may not have had any support or known of any resources. Acting as a caregiver requires superhuman strength, stamina and emotional resilience.

For anyone who has not been a caregiver, there is no way to appreciate the crushing round-the-clock responsibility, stress and relentless emotional angst. The natural end to that is a pain far worse.

CHAPTER FIFTY-ONE

ANGELS IN DISGUISE

I t's important for me to balance this story by listing some of the many blessings we received. I am certain that God provided me with exactly what I needed when I needed it. Generally, the "what" he provided were angels in disguise. Many of them.

Sometimes good friends came and stayed with Glen so that I could run errands or do some of the things I needed to do.

Ruth Harrell was an important angel. She didn't wait to be asked for help. She took initiative. She checked in with the Amyotrophic Lateral Sclerosis Association in Huntsville for ideas. An official from the ALS association provided her with a manual of helpful ideas and information, and they suggested to Ms Ruth that she be equally helpful to us both. That manual is now in the church's library.

After that, Ms Ruth rounded up volunteers. One Sunday, she announced in her Sunday school class that she wanted to form a "care team" of volunteers to help Glen and me. She asked for anyone who might be interested to see her after the class. She thought a couple of people might approach her, but she was besieged by volunteers. About ten people stepped up immediately, men and women. Some of the volunteers were people we did not even know.

Before long, we had wonderful support from people running errands, preparing meals, staying overnight to help with his physical care. Men would come by to visit with Glen and take him out of the house for drives so that he could get some fresh air. We could never have made it without those people. In fact, we could never have continued to have him living at home. We are immensely grateful.

I leaned heavily on Ms Ruth's care team, as well as my good friends and the experts from the ALS organization.

That outpouring of support came as a surprise to Jacob. "I knew that everyone liked and respected him. I had always known that. But it wasn't until he got sick and people began to step up, people I never expected to step up, that I realized how many people loved Daddy," Jacob said. He added that he was surprised by the people he "thought would step up, but who didn't."

Jacob didn't know the whole story. The fact is, everyone stepped up. But for some people, it was too painful to watch Glen waste away. They could not bear it. It's a difficult thing for anyone. It's harder for some people than for others.

Those people were the invisible volunteers who sent over meals, who ran errands, who called and asked what we needed and made sure we got it.

Some were hands-on, while others helped quietly in the background. Both groups were vital to our well-being. They provided necessary physical, medical, social, emotional and respite support. I suspect that they have no idea how important they were for us.

Ms Ruth stayed with Glen one Sunday so that I could go to church. I hadn't been in a long time. I discovered throughout the entire experience that God would provide me with precisely the measure of strength that I needed to handle the challenges of that day. For that single day, not for the day before that or for the day to come, but for that day. I had to live in the present. I had to live one day at a time.

Sometimes, angels were quite unexpected. We had been paying a lady, actually a cousin by marriage, to come clean our house every other week. Finally, I had to tell her that we could no longer afford her, because the expenses of Glen's care were so great. To my surprise, she said okay, she would still clean the house for no pay. Her gift of service was to clean, she believed. That's exactly what she did until Glen passed away. After Glen died, I told her that I could pay her again and we resumed our previous arrangement.

CHAPTER FIFTY-TWO

HIS CARE WAS INTIMIDATING

W e had turned our bedroom into a makeshift hospital room equipped with oxygen and cough-assistance machinery, which helps patients who cannot cough for themselves, and anything else that would make his life tolerable. Whitney donated a day bed, which we placed next to Glen's hospital bed where I slept. As Glen's illness progressed, caring for Glen's physical care was daunting, even for a nurse. I cannot imagine how difficult it would be for someone without medical experience. Some of the equipment was unfamiliar to me.

Glen had a cough-assist machine to help him now that he no longer had the strength to cough. He choked easily from the excessive salivation, so I had to suction him. (Shortly before he passed away, we discovered that injections of Botox would be able to help with the excessive salivation, but we discovered it much too late.)

The last few months of his life, I averaged between two and six hours of sleep each night. Six hours of sleep was a luxury. "We had to force her to take a nap," Whitney said. But even then, I couldn't sleep soundly. For good or bad, I had learned the art of hyper-vigilant sleeping; the kind that new mothers experience. I was attuned to listening to the slightest sound Glen made. During the last months of his life, he could only make grunting sounds and slow nodding of his head to indicate his needs.

CHAPTER FIFTY-THREE

GLEN'S BRAND-NEW VOICE

G len wrote emails prolifically. But emails couldn't handle every situation. One time, Glen needed to sign his name on a document at a bank. The woman helping him didn't know him, so when he had trouble speaking and signing his name she assumed that he was illiterate.

She told him to just mark an "X."

He came and told me, "She thought I was illiterate!"

She probably meant no insult, but Glen was deeply hurt.

Just because a person is disabled, it does not mean they need to be coddled like a child. Respect is extremely important to a disabled person. Dignity and respect were vitally important for Glen.

Glen was hardly a vain person or a person who needed praise, but he suffered emotionally because he lost his self-reliance. He hated his dependency. The disease dealt a blow to his sense of masculinity and his self-esteem as well as to his body. For him, the knowledge that others were doing so many things for him he used to do for himself produced a certain amount of guilt.

We wanted Glen to feel joy and purpose and peace. We needed him to know he was still the husband and the father in our family. We needed him to know that he was as important to us as he had always been. Some people shuffle a sick person off into a back room and treat them as if they are no longer a part of the family or the community. That robs the person's sense of identity and his importance in the family. That is to the detriment of everyone concerned. It's like gradually pushing someone into his grave long before his time. I can easily imagine how that treatment would erode a patient's will to live.

That is why we made sure that Glen remained involved in our family activities as much and as long as he could. We made sure Glen knew that he made his own choices about his life, his activities and his care.

The emails had been a door to the outside world, but the emails did not work for every situation. The loss of Glen's ability to speak had sharply diminished his personal interaction with people. He felt isolated, lonely, and sad. It broke my heart. Glen so thrived on the interaction with other people that the loss of his ability to communicate devastated him.

Once again, Ms Ruth arranged the solution. She helped us obtain grant money and, with some funds from the ALS Association, plus insurance, we were able to come up with the $10,000 needed to pay for a Dynavox. For those unfamiliar with it, a Dynavox is a machine that produces electronic speech. The noted physicist who also has ALS, Stephen Hawking, Ph.D., uses that type of device to communicate.

Of all the assistive devices Glen acquired, "the little talking machine," as Zac called it, was the most significant. It restored Glen's ability to communicate. There is no way to describe the difference that made to Glen's quality of life. By typing with his large toe in a slow methodical manner, the machine would produce electronic speech. The machine has a touchpad screen and translates keystrokes into speech. The machine would have been helpful during his encounter with the woman at the bank.

Glen was able to program the machine with common phrases that he might use again and again. Still the jokester, he began to have lots of fun with the machine. He made jokes or said silly things that entertained us all. When he felt playful, he called me "Old Woman!"

Sometimes the grandchildren had a little fun with the machine, too. They programed silly things into the machine and laughed at the electronic speech.

Glen's spirits soared. He had his voice back.

Ronnie fashioned a low, wheeled dolly with a lip to hold the Dynavox that Glen could push with his foot, taking it with him into whatever room he wanted to go.

At the end, he became too exhausted to use it. But for a long while, thanks to the Dynavox Glen was able to communicate and interact with people again. After Glen died, we donated the Dynavox, the rolling cart and many of the other assistive devices to the ALS association.

Bruce and Susan Lovett had a Christmas party in the early part of December that year. Glen and I went and introduced the world, or our friends at least, to Glen's new mechanical voice. It was the highlight of the evening.

Glen worked the Dynavox with his big toe the whole night. People would ask him questions that he would answer on the Dynavox .He got a bit carried away telling all sorts of things he didn't need to tell a room filled with people.

I finally told him, "If you do not shut up, I am going to unplug that machine!"

Secretly, though, I was thrilled. It was the first time in so many months that I was able to see Glen have a good time. He was back in his familiar mode of interacting with friends, joking with them. The mood was light, and people were laughing again. Long after the party, people talked about how funny he had been.

Chapter fifty-four

GLEN'S SPIN

Glen's lifelong pattern of finding humor in extraordinarily difficult situations sharpened to a fine edge as his illness progressed. In one email, sent to Toby, Glen poked fun at his need for assistance with bathing, dressing, and hygiene.

The Pampered Man's Club

By Glen Maholovich

This is for your ponderment.

Ah, the life of being spoiled rotten. I do not have to go to work, and yet I still get paid.

I stay up as late as I want and sleep to 1 p.m. every day.

I am fed three times per day, I don't even have to ask for it.

I do no dishes, laundry, grass or repairs. My clothes are not only picked out for me, but they are put on me by someone else's hands.

I have a hot rod toilet* that even takes care of me.

I have several different women to give me a shower;

I mean, what's not to love.

But before you sign up Toby, remember, that you either have to be crippled or filthy rich. Just good-looking won't cut it. But you are a shoe-in because you own your own business and everyone knows when you own your own business you have to be rich.

So I await your application.

*(His "hot-rod toilet" was a bidet.)

By this time, Glen had learned to accept his dependence on others with grace. Never did he express bitterness. Sadness that his time with us was growing short, but never bitterness.

There were old habits of his, however, that were hard for him to let go. For example, there came a time when I decided that I needed to pay someone else to cut the grass during the summer months. Glen was appalled at the thought. The idea that we would pay someone else to mow our lawn was utterly foreign to his psyche.

CHAPTER FIFTY-FIVE

THE BREAKING POINT

E ven with the help that we had, the lion's share of his care had to be mine. All of the time Glen and I were together was now relegated to meeting his basic needs.

There were no weekends off. Eventually I worked four-day weeks for my boss, Dr. Jon Yoder. However, I know that arrangement is not an option open to everyone. I was extremely fortunate.

Glen wanted only me to help him with his most intimate personal care. I understood that. My world had begun to be all about Glen's care, nothing else.

We had long since ceased any kind of interaction with each other beyond his physical care. My own identity had ceased to exist. I was physically exhausted and sleep-deprived. There was never enough time. Life moved from one urgent task to another without time in between to breathe.

"I am so discouraged, tired, down. I can feel myself sinking further down, into . . . what? Sadness, hopelessness, despair, all such negative feelings. I know as a Christian . . . I should not feel so desperate. It is so eerie, the calmness of these negative emotions. I have so little energy left. I am on the verge of tears almost constantly. So easy to anger. That's not me! But I have no control. Glen continues to weaken, though he has gained six pounds, he is still so tired. The smallest activity exhausts him. His arms continue to weaken, limiting his ability to do the simplest of things. I am so tired."

—Journal, March 19, 2010

"For an awful long time there [Vanessa] was operating on love," Maggie said. "She didn't have anything else left, physically, emotionally, mentally. She just had love. She was going to do anything and everything she had to, to help her man."

That was closer to truth than hyperbole. Glen was the love of my life. My love for Glen held me up and pushed through those difficult times.

Both Gerald and Keith spoke identical words, "I don't know how many women would have done what Vanessa did."

Bruce called me "a trooper," and remarked on the fact that I didn't complain. "She had a lot to complain about, but she never did," Bruce said.

Far from being a saintly attribute, not complaining was just practical. I had neither the time nor the energy to spare for it. I did not feel like a trooper or a hero. Despite those kind words from my friends, I did not feel as if I did anything well. I was barely hanging on by my fingernails. I knew that tenuous hold would fail at any moment.

I had moments of despair and self-doubt.

"It has been so long since my last entry. So much, yet so little has changed. The battle continues to rage. The wind blows fierce. The dark cloud of the disease continues to overshadow us. . . . Glen is progressively weaker. He can no longer lift his hands. He barely can hold his head up from his chest. He continues to have episodes of drowning in his own secretions. Leaving the house is a hardship on him and on me. He is a prisoner in his body. I, too, have become its prisoner.

I hate this disease, and what it has stolen from my husband and from us. I feel every day more a caregiver than a wife. I know that God is merciful and with us. But I am having a hard time finding Him. I feel so far removed from my God. So far removed from everything familiar. My comfortable routine has long ago ceased. I flip-flop with emotion. I want to see Glen freed. How I long to be freed. Is that selfish. Where, God, are you? Won't you please hear my cries for deliverance?

—Journal, July 14, 2011

Although he needed round the clock care, Glen strenuously resisted outside professional caretakers. He did not want "babysitters," as he referred to them. However, things were rapidly reaching yet another breaking point. Somewhere in the depths of my exhausted brain, I knew that if I did not have help, there would be two sick people in the house.

Even so, I had difficulty turning Glen's care over to other people. It felt like admitting defeat. It felt like failure. I am his wife and I am a nurse. There should be no reason I could not do this thing. I felt like I was letting him down. The one thing he had asked me to do was the one thing that was becoming impossible.

CHAPTER FIFTY-SIX

THE FAMILY MEETING

G len's physical care was not as stressful for me as the emotional struggle. His safety was a concern. My exhaustion was a concern. Either we needed him to accept the assistance of professional aides or he would need to go to a nursing home.

Ms Ruth Harrell helped me, again. "You have to focus on what's best for him. That's got to be the choice."

It became a matter of Unpleasant Choice A or Unpleasant Choice B.

Still it had to be Glen's decision. I learned to approach him with the alternatives. These were all becoming painfully difficult. None of the alternatives was palatable any more. It meant accepting that he had reached yet another disheartening milestone in his progression.

We held a family meeting. Ms Ruth, our adult children and I met with Glen to discuss the options.

I told him that if he continued to refuse care from sitters and other volunteers, we would have to put him into a nursing home. It was his choice, I told him. He relented.

Glen entered hospice care. Hospice is not a place but a concept of care, a status change. The shift in focus goes from efforts to cure a patient, to making a dying patient as comfortable as possible in his last days. In Europe, hospice care usually happens in medical facilities, but in the United States, the majority of hospice patients remain at home. Some hospice care takes place in nursing homes and occasionally in hospitals. The family continues to care for the patient and a hospice nurse makes regular visits. To be eligible for hospice care, the patient must be terminally ill or presumed likely to die within six months.

When he finally did accept the help of others into his home, he used humor to handle that as well. He used to tell people that the outside helpers were there to protect him from me.

When Glen finally agreed to let hospice aides bathe him, it freed up time for us to spend quality time together. This took a huge load off of me physically. And it gave us back a relationship.

PART SEVEN
BETWEEN TWO WORLDS

HAPPY TIMES AT THE BEACH

CHAPTER FIFTY-SEVEN

GLEN THE ENCOURAGER

By now Glen began to grow more spiritually wise in inverse proportion to the breakdown of his body. It almost seemed as if he were living in two worlds at the same time.

Our house was often crowded. On Sundays, it had been a standing habit of ours to have people drop by and have lunch with us. Of course, as Glen become more and more ill, we couldn't do that, but people still came by and visited. People didn't just visit on Sundays. Glen loved being with people and they loved being with him. Glen would sit at the table talking in his own way with people until he could no longer sit at the table. After that, people would take turns going in to his room to visit with him.

No matter how sick he was, people wanted to be around him.

Our granddaughter Ansleigh put it like this: "There were always so many people!"

People continued to gravitate toward him even though he was becoming harder to understand. In latter months, Glen's comments were delayed as he typed them on his Dynavox with his toe.

Glen made people feel good whenever they were around him. He wanted to hear about what was going on in their lives. He wasn't interested in talking about himself, but he would if someone asked and really wanted to know. He much preferred to hear about them.

"Glen was real. He was transparent. He was comfortable in his own skin. He didn't try to impress anyone. He never lost his joy. He always had something funny to say and he was always an encourager. People wanted to hear whatever he had to say. He was just that kind of person," Keith Lisenby said.

"He never gave up; he never lost his sense of humor."

Glen loved to laugh and he loved to hear other people laugh. Glen lived every moment of his life more fully than many able-bodied people do.

"We would just sit there at the kitchen table and listen to him," said Keith, who spent many hours there. "I've seen many, many people, who are very sick get discouraged and despondent because of the position they are in. Glen never did."

People sought his wisdom even if he himself doubted he had any wisdom to offer. He was loving. He was interesting. He was insightful. He was filled with life experience. He was kind. He was funny. He was comforting and he was inspirational. Glen seemed to be the only person unaware of those qualities in himself. He wanted people around him to be happy. It was important to him to lift other people's spirits, even when they had dropped by specifically to comfort him and lift his spirits.

There was a breast cancer survivor, Louise Brogden, in our town. She was a dietitian who was extremely helpful in trying to come up with the proper nutrients to feed Glen in the proper amounts through the PEG tub. She told us the story about a particular visit she paid to Glen.

One day she woke with a strong sense that she ought to go visit Glen. Her plan was to visit him, keep him company and to say comforting, encouraging things to him. That's the reason we visit sick people, isn't it?

I am sure her visit did comfort Glen. But when she told the story to us, she said Glen somehow managed to reverse the scenario. He was the one who did the comforting and encouraging. She left feeling as if she was the one who had been helped. We heard stories like that all the time.

It was the same for both Debbie and Keith. They visited always intending to lift Glen's spirits, but inevitably, they left feeling like the ones whose spirits had been lifted.

"He had not been able to drink on his own or feed himself or even go to the bathroom by himself, and anyone else would have felt sorry for themselves, but he never did," Debbie said. "He was always so encouraging. That's just not something you see very often."

Glen's tendency to comfort and encourage seemed to bubble up from inside him.

"One day Debbie and I told him that we were thinking of going into the ministry," Keith said, "and Glen got very excited. We could see that he was happy and proud for us. He typed the words out on his little machine, but we would have known he was thrilled for us, anyway. It was all over his face."

Glen was optimistic, but he had a fearless candor that left people with no doubt that he genuinely felt and believed whatever he said. He didn't know how to be false. It would never have occurred to him to say things to impress people.

Those observations about Glen were universal.

"He was always forthcoming and candid. I would go to him to ask him questions about life situations and he gave me answers that were filled with wisdom," Keith said.

"Glen didn't give advice. He made suggestions based on his experience and he asked questions that made you think," Keith said. Glen suggested that Keith and Debbie avoid burnout in their church work. He stressed that. "Don't burn yourself out," Glen told them. Burnout could affect their energy and the quality of their service. "When you wear yourself out, you don't have anything to give anyone else."

The couple did enter the ministry.

Glen's positive outlook was evident in practically everything he did and said, including his own mistakes. He turned negatives into positives. He talked about that to Keith. Glen often told people that he had faults, that he had made lots of mistakes. He would say that he had made bad decisions in his life.

But Glen believed that mistakes could be made beneficial as a teaching tool. He believed a mistake could be transformed into something positive.

"You're going to make mistakes," Glen said. "That's human. The mistake is not what matters. What matters is how you deal with that mistake afterward."

He demonstrated rather than advocated. "He was humble. He was so talented and had done so much, but he never sought accolades. He never wanted that. He was a man of such genuine character," Keith said

People often avoid sick people, out of fear or discomfort, or uncertainty of what to say or how to help, or from the pain of watching someone they care about slipping away from them. People didn't avoid Glen. They embraced his friendship. People respected Glen's wisdom and sought it out.

"Other people in life look up to athletes, celebrities or financially successful people as role models, but I looked up to Glen," Keith said. "Glen had more of what I wanted than any of those types of people." We heard that kind of comment often, too.

Susan gratefully listened to Glen as well. "Shiny objects in life can so easily distract us, but Glen's circumstances and his acceptance of them showed us what is important in your life — relationships and the time that we have to spend together. I just wouldn't take anything for the time I had with Glen," she said.

Going through something like this makes you so acutely aware of how precious every moment in life is, she said. Watching someone else go through it with such incredible grace does that, too.

"Glen was fearless in the way that he handled this thing; how he was able to cope with this," Susan said. "He never, ever gave up the fight. That's what was so remarkable. This was definitely a brand-new experience for me. I have been around other people who were dying, and they give up. But this was a new experience and it was so refreshing."

Keith talked about how Glen encouraged them to pursue their own dream. "He encouraged us, he cheered our dreams, he comforted and he applauded our successes. There was no question in our minds that he loved us, as we loved him," Keith said. "Even when he couldn't speak the words, it was obvious on his face."

"There had to be times when Glen was despondent, but he tried to prevent anyone seeing that. In most cases, his sadness was not so much about his imminent death as it was about his inability to do some of the things he once could do, which he considered his gifts to his family and his community. He felt sadness about the effect that his illness and his care had on his family. And he felt sadness about leaving them too soon. The way he talked about his family and the way that he looked at them and they interacted with such good humor and kidding around with one another. He left his mark and it was a good one.

"There were moments when he worried much about his family. Not worried about whether his family would be all right without him, but he worried that he was letting them down," Keith said.

"He talked to me a lot about Vanessa. He said a couple of times that he felt like he had let Vanessa down."

Keith assured him he had not. He also told Glen that his friends would be here to help me.

"When he fell on Christmas Eve, I went up to the emergency room where they were. So many people were there, on Christmas Eve. There is no doubt that he was in pain, but he wouldn't show it. Glen was laughing and cutting up. He didn't want all his friends and family to worry and see him suffer. You could see and feel the love in the room. The time that we spent with him, this whole situation is one that I have never experienced in my life, and it was one of the most rewarding and valuable times in my life," Keith said.

Keith helped officiate at Glen's funeral.

CHAPTER FIFTY-EIGHT

"TO MY WIFE, VANESSA"

For years, long before Glen's illness, we had planned to celebrate our thirty-fifth anniversary with a cruise to Alaska. However, we both knew now that would not be possible. We had both accepted that, so when the anniversary came around I expected an ordinary celebration. It was customary at our church for the pastor to announce anniversaries and birthdays from the pulpit. So when ours came, I was not terribly surprised when the pastor announced ours.

But then he asked for the two of us to stand facing one another and join hands. Because Glen could no longer speak, a church friend, Richard Keesler, stood at the pulpit and began reading a special letter Glen had written to me.

To my wife, Vanessa:

Thirty-five years ago, you made a promise to me . . . to love me for richer or poorer, in sickness and in health. When you made that promise, we thought we could conquer the world and felt like we would live forever. There was a time in our life that all we had was love . . . we are there again. You have proven your love in many ways, but I think the greatest started almost six years ago. God is leading us down a path that we must walk in faith daily. I have never doubted that you were the wife that God planned for me to have. I want you to know. I not only love you, but I praise and thank you for your love and faithfulness to me. I pray God bless you in every aspect of your life.

With love, I say Happy 35th Anniversary

From your husband, Glen

Every single one of us knew that this was so much more than a quick sit-down dash-it-off kind of letter. We knew the incredible effort it took. We knew that every individual letter, every comma, every space between words had been a monumental effort. And we all knew the complicated arrangements he had made to surprise me.

No gift to any wife has ever been more romantic than that one.

CHAPTER FIFTY-NINE

WHITNEY'S BIRTHDAY

Whitney's birthday came about two weeks before Glen died. Of course we didn't know his death would happen when it did, but we knew that we wouldn't have him much longer. We all wanted to have Glen share in her birthday and in another surprise, one Whitney didn't know about.

Whitney had her heart set on a little pink pistol. She had been talking about it and she was convinced that's what Jacob would give her for her birthday.

Surely, Glen would want to be a part of that. He was thoroughly fascinated that this petite young woman with such a sweet disposition was a cop who carried a gun.

In order to include Glen, Whitney's mom had put together a birthday dinner for her at our house. We told Whitney we would celebrate her birthday and then watch the Alabama game. Our daughter had already told Whitney she would not be able to make it to the party. Whitney's dad couldn't make it, either.

She was surprised when she got to the house and found Jacob's sister and the grandchildren there, after all. The little ones kept trying to get Whitney to open one particular gift that we wanted her to open in front of Glen.

We all crowded into Glen's room. Jacob told Whitney to sit down on the bed right next to Glen. Suddenly the small bedroom filled with more people. Whitney was shocked to see her father walk into the room.

Jacob handed Whitney a Cracker-Jack bag. She opened it and inside she saw a small plastic container, such as the kind that come from a gumball machine. She shook it and saw a bright, shining object inside. When she looked down, Jacob was on one knee.

She looked at Glen. She looked at each one of us turn and finally she looked at Jacob on his knee. She was so surprised that she didn't speak. Our daughter broke the silence. "Well, are you going to say yes, or are you just going to sit there?"

Then Glen, who had known the plan ahead of time, cracked a smile and everybody started laughing and crying. Whitney did say "Yes." Whitney did not get her pink pistol that day, but she has one now.

Glen asked when we thought the wedding would be. It would be after Jacob graduated. Glen dropped his head because he knew he wouldn't be there. It was heartbreakingly clear he wished he could attend the wedding.

Jacob and Whitney said that they would get married sooner, but Glen wouldn't have it. "He told us in no uncertain terms that we were not to live our lives around him and his illness," Whitney said. "If he had not told us that, we would have done it. I think, in a way, he was letting us go."

"We knew, and he knew, that he wouldn't make it to the wedding, but we at least were able to have him there for the engagement," Whitney said. Glen passed away just ten days later.

When Jacob and Whitney began talking about getting married, Glen spoke with Whitney's father privately to make a special request. He told Whitney's father that Jacob would need a father. He asked Whitney's father to stand in for him as Jacob's father after he was gone.

"I know that it must have been very painful for Glen to ask someone else to do that," Whitney said.

Glen had started sending Whitney emails. "He wanted me to know that Jacob and the kids were fortunate to have one more person in their corner," Whitney said. "One of the last emails he sent me welcomed me into the family. He said he believed I was going to make Jacob happy."

"My biggest regret is that I don't have a picture of Glen with me when he was healthy that I could put up in the house," she said.

Chapter sixty

PERSPECTIVE

The disease robbed Glen of his ability to be the grandfather he wished to be. The former high school star athlete could not toss a toy football to his grandson. The family all worried that children Whitney and Jacob might have would never know Glen. Our grandson, Keaton, was only about two and a half when Glen died, so he has little memory of him.

In fact, I worried about what Glen's illness would do to this innocent toddler. Day after day, the child watched his grandfather's condition deteriorate. I worried about what the experience would do to all the grandchildren.

One day I saw that tiny child grasping the finger of his ailing grandfather to lead him from the bathroom back to his bedroom. Some friends, who had brought over some food, were looking on as well.

That's when my internal rage came to a boil. It was so horribly unfair. To all of us. To Glen, to Keaton, to me and the entire family. It was too much.

Glen was still able to ambulate to the bathroom with the assistance of two or three people. His gait was slow and shuffling and the process exhausted him, but he desperately wished to maintain whatever scrap of dignity that he could. Several people were assisting him back to his bed, including this child.

Silently — but if thoughts could scream, my thoughts were screaming — I began to read God the riot act. All I could think about was how under ordinary circumstances Glen would be running around chasing Keaton, laughing and tossing him a toy football. Oh, how Glen would have loved that!

Glen should not be a bed-bound invalid taking help from a two-year-old. It went against everything that seemed right. It was simply too unfair.

I was still engrossed in my mental tirade toward God, when my visiting friend's sweet voice disrupted my anger.

"What did you say?" I asked her.

"Look at them," she repeated. "There they are, these grandchildren, already learning about service." She motioned with her head toward Keaton holding his grandfather's finger.

I saw, in that instant, how distorted my perspective had been. I was seeing only the downside of the situation. My dear friend with her gentle observation showed me how to see things with a different perspective. In all bad, something good can be found, if we are willing to see it.

CHAPTER SIXTY-ONE

NECK BRACE AND BOTOX

Toward what we now know was the end of his life, Glen had trouble holding his head up. Someone got the idea that a neck brace might help. That sounded like a perfectly reasonable idea.

Bruce took Glen to Mobile to get him a neck brace. He was fitted and they headed for home, with Glen wearing the brace.

As they were traveling down the road, Glen started choking.

The choking was horrifying. And it wasn't stopping on its own as it normally did.

It shook the unflappable Bruce.

"That is the closest I have ever come to panicking," Bruce said. "I didn't know exactly what to do. I was trying to hold him up with my right hand, and drive with my left hand." As a retired law enforcement officer, Bruce had some experience with driving emergencies. However, this was unnerving in a way he hadn't anticipated.

It turned out that the brace itself was preventing Glen from leaning his head forward to ease the spasm as he normally did. They managed to remove the neck brace and eventually the choking spasm passed. Glen was just as shaken as Bruce had been. That was the one and only time he ever wore it.

For some time, I secretly worried that Glen would die a horrible frightening death by choking. The nagging fear distressed me so much that I finally approached the doctor I work for to ask him directly what he thought would happen. What I wanted was his reassurance that my fear was unfounded.

I asked him if he would give me his professional opinion about what would be the likely manner of Glen's death. Specifically, I asked him if Glen would choke to death.

"Oh, Vanessa, that's not what's going to happen," my doctor told me. Fortunately, he backed up his statement, so that I knew he wasn't just trying to ease my worry. He explained the process to me in specific clinical terms that I could understand. Glen's diaphragm was paralyzed. That meant that carbon dioxide build up would be the eventual cause of his death. He would likely pass away in his sleep. As it turned out, that is exactly how it happened. I will be forever grateful for that.

Glen never lost his sense of humor. He joked with people almost to his last breath. Bruce and Susan Lovett took one last trip with us shortly before Glen's death. We went to Atlanta to get Botox injections for Glen. Susan's mother had been going to Atlanta to get injections for a throat ailment. At that point, Glen was salivating a great deal, and that prompted his choking. We thought that maybe if he got injections of Botox it might control the excessive salivation.

Glen could no longer control his arms and legs. Bruce would help Glen out of the car by giving him a great big bear hug, and then place him into the wheelchair. Because he was not able to speak so that most people could understand him, I acted as his translator. Glen whispered a comical jab for me to pass on. "Tell Bruce to quit squeezing me so hard!'"

It turned out that the Botox injections worked. I wish we had tried that earlier.

CHAPTER SIXTY-TWO

HALFWAY HOME

As death appeared more imminent, Glen's tone, his sense of acceptance, changed. He began slowly moving into another life. He became a man living simultaneously in both the physical world here and the spiritual world of heaven.

Glen was fearless.

Susan Lovett remembers his incredible courage in the face of adversity, "If he felt any fear or had any fear, I never saw it. I'm sure there had to be times when he was depressed, but I never saw that depression myself. He displayed such incredible courage and humor."

We knew that he didn't want to die; just that he accepted it and was prepared for it. He was so very tired. It grieved him to leave his family. But he was utterly unafraid of death.

In one of his emails to Toby, he wrote:

"My faith in God has grown even though my physical body has steadily grown worse. I search through scriptures for my answers and I know without a doubt that God is my answer in this life and in the next. Maggie sent me an email, about a little boy who died and went to heaven that encouraged me so much. You see, sometimes in my mind I am more alive in that world than I am in this world."

"I have never seen somebody going through the dying process who was still so kind and gracious. Glen was not a bit worried about dying. He was only worried about Vanessa, and his children, and his grandchildren, and of course his friends. It was clear to me that he was positive he was going to heaven," Maggie said.

"Glen was worried about his family in the present and in the future. For the present, he was worried about the level of stress and heartache his illness was causing them. It was so difficult for Glen to bear anyone else's discomfort in his presence."

One day Glen asked me to promise him that I would never put him on a ventilator.

He had no idea how hard that would be for me. I knew that I might not have the emotional strength to keep such a promise. I asked Glen to put his wishes in writing, so that I would have a legal document, his living will, to brace my emotional resistance, in order to follow his wishes. I promised him that I would abide by his wishes if he drew up a living will. He did that. A living will is a tremendous gesture of kindness for loved ones and Glen gave me that kindness.

Everyone called him courageous. Inspirational. Gracious.

And he was every single one of those things, even though he didn't think so. Humility, which he didn't recognize either, was one of his most endearing qualities.

If it took all the strength he had, Glen insisted on showing respect, gratitude and friendship. He wanted his visitors to know that he was glad to see them. Maggie went to see Glen just a day or two before he died.

When Glen saw Maggie, he struggled to raise himself up to see her.

"It took all that he had just to do that," she said. "He was having trouble communicating, but I knew that he was trying very hard to tell me that he loved me."

CHAPTER SIXTY-THREE

GOODBYE, I LOVE YOU

The subconscious awareness that my time with Glen was growing short became the catalyst that kept me going when I wanted to collapse. Whether I allowed myself to admit it or not, I knew it in my heart it was the twilight of our days together. It no longer mattered how exhausted or brokenhearted I was. That's not true, of course. It mattered, but my needs were an icicle alongside the iceberg of my husband's needs. I have no explanation for what enabled me to accomplish what I did. The only strength I had left was God's help and my love for Glen. The generous, loving help of family and friends most certainly saved my sanity.

Glen could no longer express his needs or wishes, but just as a mother understands the meaning of each facial expression, a slightly raised eyebrow, a squint or the tone and resonance of her infant's cry, I had learned the meaning of each of Glen's grunts and sounds. He was so incredibly fragile. I was extremely protective. I was now a mother bear tending to my ailing mate.

CHAPTER SIXTY-FOUR

EVERY WORD BUT *THAT* WORD

Without saying the word "goodbye," Glen told each of his friends and family goodbye, one by one. Glen sent private, sometimes lengthy, heartfelt emails to people whom he regarded with deep affection. Glen had been clandestinely finishing his goodbyes to those he loved, without telling anyone what he was doing.

He said goodbye to Whitney in one of those emails, although she didn't realize until later that he was telling her goodbye. He wrote to her with warmth to welcome her to the family, and he told her that he knew Jacob would be faithful to her. He told her that he knew Whitney would make Jacob and his children very happy.

Glen never used the word "goodbye" in that email. Glen would not say goodbye to anyone he loved; only "I love you."

By this time, Glen could not communicate at all. His exhaustion had taken over and even his talking machine was too exhausting. It broke Glen's heart that his loved ones couldn't grasp the meaning of his attempts at speech.

Glen desperately tried to express something to Ronnie several times, but Ronnie could not understand what he was trying to say. It seemed important to Glen that Ronnie understand. The look on his face each time Ronnie couldn't understand him was a look of deep pain," Ronnie said. "If I had to guess, I think what he said was, 'I love you.' I believe that's what he said."

I know that is what he said. I have no doubt, whatsoever, that Glen said exactly those words to Ronnie. For one thing, he truly did love Ronnie. And by this time, he was making sure to tell the people he loved that he did love them, even though we didn't catch on to the fact at the time.

The very last words he said to me were, "I love you," our daughter said. That was three days before he died, when it was clear that he had little time left. She had previously written him an email to say how much she loved him, and to let him go. She made it clear she hadn't given up *all* hope of a recovery for him, but that she was reconciled to the possibility of his death.

"You are an amazing dad . . . I can't wait to see you healed, talking and giving me a big bear hug.

And even if I have to wait an eternity to see it, I will be there! I love you very much."

During one conversation, Bruce did most of the talking. Bruce made it clear to Glen that his family would be safe and protected, that he would make sure of that.

Bruce wanted Glen to know it was okay for him to stop fighting, that it was all right for Glen to rest.

"I reassured him that I would look out for his family and that he didn't have to hang on. He was so tired and he fought so hard," Bruce told him. "By that time, we knew that death would be a blessing for him."

CHAPTER SIXTY-FIVE

I HOPE YOU DANCE

Glen said goodbye to me two different times.

He said his first, verbal goodbye, without using that word, shortly before he died. We were in the kitchen talking. He suddenly got very serious. He looked me straight in the eyes and told me to live my life and be happy.

"I want you to move on with your life. I want you to be happy. I want you to go places, experience things, do things that you want to do, to laugh," he said.

He was telling me that I should not live in perpetual mourning of his memory. He was telling me to live my later life without sadness or guilt. It was clear to me that it was important for him to know that I would be happy after he was gone.

His words reminded me of the beautiful song recorded by Lee Ann Womack called, "I Hope You Dance."

These words from the song remind me of that conversation:

I HOPE YOU DANCE

I hope you never lose your sense of wonder,

You get your fill to eat but always keep that hunger,

May you never take one single breath for granted,

GOD forbid love ever leave you empty handed,

I hope you still feel small when you stand beside the ocean,

Whenever one door closes I hope one more opens,

Promise me that you'll give faith a fighting chance,

And when you get the choice to sit it out or dance.

I hope you dance . . . I hope you dance

When I hear the song, I think of Glen. I think of what he said to me. Once again, he had given me an incredible, selfless gift. He wanted me to be happy after he was gone. He wanted me to dance again. I hope I do. That may be more difficult to do than it sounds.

CHAPTER SIXTY-SIX

THE POWER OF SILENCE

An illness that strips away your ability to speak and to move requires some ingenuity to communicate. For a time — before he lost nearly all the ability to move — we had been able to communicate with gestures. But even that fell away as his disease ravaged his body.

We had one last heart-to-heart conversation in nearly complete silence.

I sat beside his bed, facing him propped up by pillows to prevent his falling over. I was extremely tired that day. I was so thoroughly exhausted, so spent, that I could no longer stifle my breaking heart. My emotional dam broke. Suddenly, it was as though every emotion I held back for so many months gushed forth all at once.

A tear fell. Then more tears fell. And many more. The tears became rivers running down my face, and I was sobbing as I have never sobbed before. A pain in my chest resulted from the inability of my tears to fall fast enough.

I started telling him how much I loved him, with such urgency; it was as if I had never told him that before.

My anguish was unbearable.

I looked at him through my tears and saw that he was silently weeping.

I so desperately longed for his arms to wrap around me as they used to. I missed that feeling of strength and security he had always provided. Of course, that could not happen, so I encircled his frail body with my arms. I kissed his face. I began again to tell him how much I loved him and to thank him for being a wonderful husband, a wonderful father to our children and a wonderful best friend and companion.

His tear-filled eyes looked directly into mine. Both of our hearts were breaking.

Slowly my tears subsided and I sat back down.

When I did, I felt his toe on my leg. He began moving it slowly up and down along my leg, achieving the only caress his body could still manage — with his toe.

He caressed my left calf, moving up and down. His eyes never left mine. I cannot imagine any soul on earth has experienced a more romantic, loving gesture from anyone.

We were saying good-bye.

CHAPTER SIXTY-SEVEN

GLEN BOARDS THE TRAIN

Whitney decided to stay close to her office on the day that Glen died, sensing that he was nearing the end. "For some reason I decided not to go to lunch with the people I work with, and I stayed at the office," Whitney said. "Every time the phone rang, I was just on pins and needles."

You don't know that the last day of someone's life is the last day, until it happens. It was a couple of days before Thanksgiving and I came home at lunchtime to place a turkey in the oven to warm up for our office Thanksgiving dinner. I was mentally ticking off a multitude of tasks I needed to do. I was tired and harried. At work, the office was filled with patients who had to be seen before the long holiday weekend.

I had a long list of errands to run. I planned to go straight back to work without stopping to say hello to Glen. I chatted briefly with Brenda, who was staying with him that day.

For some reason just before I left, I stopped and went in to speak to him. He was propped up with pillows into a seated position at the side of his bed. Glen looked quite bewildered to see me at home in the middle of the day. For quite a long time he had been unable to speak, so my only way to discern his thoughts was to read the expression on his face and look into his eyes. Now, his eyes were inquisitive. They seemed to say, "What are you doing at home at this time of the day?"

I explained to him why I was there. Then I leaned over and kissed his forehead. I told him that I loved him, and then I went back to work.

I hadn't been back at work long when the hospice nurse called me to say that something was very wrong with Glen. She told me she had dropped in to see Glen and had found him unresponsive. She had tried and tried, but she could not rouse him. She asked me to try to get a doctor and come home right away. Immediately, I went to the examining room where Dr. Yoder was seeing a patient and waited anxiously outside. I told him what the hospice nurse said and asked him to please come with me to visit Glen. He followed me home.

We found Glen exactly as I had left him, propped up by the pillows. However, now he was unconscious. He was breathing, but his breathing had changed. I tried repeatedly to get him to respond to my voice, but he never did. I knew that Glen was dying.

The doctor and the hospice nurse didn't need to tell me that. I probably would have known even if I weren't a nurse. All my nursing experience was no help at all to accept that this man I had desperately loved most of my life was slipping so utterly out of my life.

Glen was on his train, nearing his last stop.

He would soon step down onto the station platform where the loved ones before him would greet him. By the time he died, he had been so very, very tired. It may have been the best thing for Glen, but it felt like the worst thing in the world for me.

CHAPTER SIXTY-EIGHT

GLEN ARGUES WITH GOD

Word spread quickly that Glen was near death. So many people began arriving at the house; soon there was scarcely air enough to breathe. I told people that if they wished they could go into his room and say good-bye and many of them did. The tiny room was crammed with people. I don't know how many were in this house, but it was clear that he was beloved. People wanted to be with Glen. They weren't there for this physical human being as much as they were there to mark his transposition from physical to spiritual. They were there to say good-bye to the spirit of this man."

We stood in the room where Glen had stopped breathing. But Glen's lion heart did not stop beating. The room was so still, so somber. The silence was thick with heavy hearts. It seemed as if we all had frozen in that moment.

Finally, after a bit, Jacob spoke up, shattering the stillness. "I know what's going on," he said. We all listened intently. "Daddy's made it up to heaven, and God is telling him where to go, and Daddy is pleading with God. 'Please don't put me where Doris is!'"

At that, the room exploded with laughter. Oh, how Glen would have loved that laughter. It relieved the tension. My mother had been colorful, to put it nicely.

Glen Maholovich died at 4:22 p.m., November 22, 2011.

When he died, people who loved him, who had learned from him, surrounded him. Glen simply wouldn't have acknowledged his incredible value to our lives.

But that's okay. Okay, because we all did.

Let no one tell you that grief is easy, or that it passes quickly. They are no instruction books. Sure, there are books about grieving, but that one definitive honest-to-goodness book that lists action steps 1-2-3 to take, to remove the pain and to re-design your life, doesn't exist.

There is a gaping, aching hole in my heart. Even in a crowd of family, friends or strangers, I feel as if there is a part of me that is missing. Every family event, whether it is a ballgame, a recital, a holiday, there is an empty seat. Occasionally, without prompting, out of nowhere, one of the grandchildren in their beautiful innocence will ask, "Do you think Bo is watching us today?" They want to know if he saw us at the beach, the bowling alley, or the ball game. We so long for him to be a part of our lives.

I always tell them that of course he is watching us and that he wants, more than he could want anything in the world, for all of us to be happy.

And I have no doubt at all that he is watching.

I have no doubt that he will be waiting and smiling when each of our railroad cars pull into that station, one by one. He'll be healthy. He'll be strong. He'll be laughing. Of course he will be laughing. He will hug us and then he will lead us all to a table piled high with great big steaks, fresh-squeezed lemonade to drink and mountains of ice cream for dessert.

CHAPTER SIXTY-NINE

AFTERWARDS

After Glen died, Keith Lisenby told us that we hadn't wlost Glen. "Glen was promoted," he said. His thoughts of Glen include a vision of him strong and healthy and eating ice cream. I began to understand that God had not ignored our prayers for Glen's healing. In fact, God did heal Glen. What God did not do was to allow the healed Glen to continue to live with us here on earth."

Toby was much too ill to help us select a casket.

But it turned out that Glen's casket presented itself to us.

When we went into the room where they have all the caskets, Jacob looked at one and said, "That's it!" And we all knew that he was right. It was exactly perfect for Glen.

It was made of the kind of wood Glen loved to use, a gorgeous oak. And it was in a style that Glen would have liked. He would not have liked the price. The cost would have sent Glen through the roof, but this time he wasn't the one paying for it.

We bought that casket. "There were about a thousand people I shook hands with at the funeral," our grandson Zac said. "I never saw so many people."

We buried him in his hometown of Bratt, Florida.

Jacob graduated college in 2012, with a degree in criminal justice, the summer after Glen died. His post on Facebook that a very important person was absent from the ceremony prompted more tears.

Not too long after Glen's death, Bobby called me. He needed to talk to someone. "Glen is not here," he said. "I usually talk to Glen about stuff like this. But he isn't here." He asked me if he could talk to me instead. He was only half-joking. I thought, *Oh, I hope, I hope, it's not anything to do with building something, because I won't know what to say.*

Immediately after Glen's death, I was able to distract myself with Jacob and Whitney's wedding plans. Jacob and Whitney were married in 2013. The wedding was bittersweet. Planning it gave me some happy thoughts. We all were so happy for Jacob and Whitney, but Glen's absence was so palpable. We didn't try to pretend otherwise. We placed Glen into the wedding symbolically. We lit memory candles in his honor. We used a beautiful arbor that Glen had built for our daughter. These words established his presence:

"Over ten years ago, a daughter asked her father to build the arbor you see here. Today, that father's son is getting married under that arbor. That father is Joseph Glen Maholovich, and though he is not with us physically, he is everywhere — in his handiwork; in the memories of his beloved wife, children and family members; in the faces of his grandchildren and in the hearts and minds of all of you that were blessed to have known him. The memory candles lit prior to the ceremony represent Glen's light that still shines in our lives. Since there are no tears in heaven, we like to believe that our heavenly Father is giving Glen a view of today's celebration while he stands tall and strong with a huge grin on his face! Thank you for being a part of our special day.

— Whitney, Jacob and the McGill and Maholovich families

I knew my life would be different without Glen, but frankly, I had been much too busy and preoccupied to give that much thought. Now I am having to re-invent my life without him.

I have embarked on yet another unwanted detour for which I am ill prepared. Only this time, Glen is not sharing the path with me. The learning curve on this is also very steep. Maybe steeper than the previous one.

I wonder if it would have been easier to start all over again in a new city, where nothing reminds me of Glen. Now, for the first time since I was fourteen years old, I am oddly single. It was two years after his death before I began to emerge from my chronic state of bewildered shock. It is still difficult to ambulate through life naturally without Glen. It's like a part of your body or your soul or your heart is missing.

The anniversary of Glen's death the next year fell on Thanksgiving. Several family birthdays also fall during that time. We all decided we didn't want to associate loss with that time. To help us shift our thinking, we celebrate Thanksgiving and Christmas in very unconventional ways, ways as far removed from thoughts of Glen's death as possible. That first anniversary, we went out to eat and then we all went bowling.

I know that I need help to work through my grief. I am seeing a counselor. I attend support group meetings with other widows. I am one of the youngest in the group. I am also attending grief classes.

Most people who grieve discover that it's the second year — the year after the support begins to drift away and the numbness and shock wear off — that is the most painful.

I will take my journey on my own, but I will not be alone. I have God, my family and friends. And I have absolute faith that a day will come when I can remember Glen without pain and without tears, but only with a smile on my face.

EPILOGUE

"**D**oes this mean you don't love my Bo anymore," was the straight from the heart question Ella, now nine, asked when I shared the news that Barry and I were going to marry.

Truthfully I had ask myself similar questions. Could I love again? Did loving again diminish the love Glen and I shared? I love Glen, always will love him. So how could I love someone else?

My answer came through the love I have for my two children. I love them equally, yet differently. Each one holds a solitary place in my heart that only be held by that child.

I explained to Ella that our hearts are large and capable of loving multiple others. And once we love no one can remove that person from that place in our heart. It is forever theirs!

I started writing this book a few months after Glen's death. By the time this book is published Glen will be gone almost four years.

I met a wonderful man eighteen months ago and fell in love with him. We married this past July surrounded by our families and close friends.

I thank God for second chances. For creating us to move on with life, to love again. The first time I met Barry the song, "I Hope You Dance," by Lee Ann Womack played on the radio. I took it as a sign. Glen had given me a wonderful gift. The gift of releasing me to live, to move on, to love again, to dance!

Vanessa Maholovich Carden resides in Tuscaloosa, AL with her husband Barry Carden.

CAREGIVER AND GRIEF SUPPORT ADVICE AND RESOURCES

S tatistics and medical and technical information within the book were obtain from the following sources, which also provide a vast array of information, fact sheets, answers to commonly asked questions and links to other resources for anyone. Arranged according to their relevance to this book.

NATIONAL ALLIANCE FOR CAREGIVING
http:// www. caregiving. org/

ALS ASSOCIATION
http:// www. Alsa.org/als-care/caregivers/

SHARE THE CARE
(How to organize a group to help.)
http:// www. sharethecare.org

CAREGIVERS OF VETERANS
http:// www. caregiver.va.gov/
Hotline: 855-260-3274

NATIONAL HOSPICE AND PALLIATIVE CARE ORGANIZATION
http:// www. nhpco.org

NATIONAL CAREGIVERS LIBRARY
http:// www. caregiverslibrary.org

ROUNDUP OF CAREGIVERS' RESOURCES
www. usa.gov/Citizen/Topics/Health/caregivers.shtm

THE UNPREPARED CAREGIVER
http:// www. unpreparedcaregiver.com/

GUIDE TO MINIMIZE CAREGIVER STRESS

• Find at least one confidante—someone close but not directly impacted—who will support you when you cry or yell or will give you a hug when you need one.

• Keep a journal.

• Know your physical, practical, and emotional limits. Clarify them to yourself and communicate them to everyone involved.

• Support and encourage your loved one's independence.

• Tell people what you need. Others cannot read your mind.

• Take advantage of community services, such as adult day care centers, home health aides, home-delivered meals, respite care, transportation services, and skilled nursing.

• Do not isolate. Nurture your close relationships and let them nurture you. Use your telephone and email, but make sure to leave the house and visit friends in person.

• Schedule daily communication with your loved one, just an email, a text, a quick phone call.

• Decide what you can realistically accomplish, and enlist friends, family, and professionals to help with the rest.

• Pray, meditate, walk on the beach, go horseback riding. Do something restorative to your soul.

• Your own good health is critical. Be faithful about keeping your own medical and dental appointments. Do not skip meals. Avoid alcohol and mind-altering substances. Sleep when you can.

ABOUT GRIEF

• Don't be surprised by the intensity of your grief.

• There is no "standard" period for grieving, though if it seems to continue too long, seek counseling. You aren't crazy, but you are in great pain.

• Grief is typically worse the second year after the loss.

• Grief isn't linear. It will ebb and flow. It will flip flop through the various, in no particular order.

• Depths of grief depend upon the relationship, its length, and circumstances of the death.

• Humor helps.

• Grief support groups or programs help.

• Therapy can help.

• Isolation may feel comfortable, but it can make your grief harder to manage.

• Starting a new long-term project that is unrelated to the loss helps.

• Add new activities, join new clubs, make new friends not associated with your lost loved one helps.

• Savor and nurture your supportive relationships.

• Trust the soft, quiet voice in your heart about decisions, not the loud, hurting voice in your head.

• Avoid mood-altering substances.

• Be honest with your friends and family about what they can do to help and what they do that doesn't help.

• Write a letter to your lost loved one.

• Do not feel you must grieve to keep your loved one's memory alive. Instead, join a cause in his or her honor.

• Don't avoid thinking about your loss, but if you get stuck, change the subject in your heart by going out, seeing a friend, taking language classes.

• Find new ways to celebrate special occasions that otherwise remind you of your loss.

• Be patient with yourself.

• Trust your instincts.

GRIEF ASSISTANCE

GRIEFSHARE SUPPORT GROUPS
PO Box 1739
Wake Forest, NC 27588
800-395-5755
www.griefshare.org

How to Help Others Who Are Grieving
www.helpguide.org

NATIONAL HOSPICE AND PALLIATIVE CARE ORGANIZATION
http:// www.nhpco.org/resources/grief-and-bereavemente.org/mental/helping_grieving.htm

GriefNet.org
Internet community of people dealing with grief, death, and major loss.
www.griefnet.org

ALS ASSOCIATION

1275 K Street, NW

Suite 1050

Washington, DC 20005

202-407-8580

http:// www.alsa.org

Email: advocacy@alsanatonal.org

AMERICAN ACADEMY OF HOSPICE AND PALLIATIVE MEDICINE

4700 W. Lake Avenue

Glenview, IL 60025-1485

Ph: 847-375-4712

Fax: 877-734-8671

http://www.aahpm.org

info@aahpm.org

MUSCULAR DYSTROPHY ASSOCIATION

USA NATIONAL HEADQUARTERS

3300 E. Sunrise Drive

Tucson, AZ 85718

http://als.mda.org/

CENTERS FOR DISEASE CONTROL AND PREVENTION, NATIONAL CENTER FOR HEALTH STATISTICS

http://www.cdc.gov/nchs/

NATIONAL ALLIANCE FOR CARE GIVING

Non-profit coalition of over 50 national organizations

4720 Montgomery Lane, 2nd Floor

Bethesda, MD 20814

http://www.caregiving.org/

Email: info@caregiving.org

AMERICAN AUTOIMMUNE RELATED DISEASES ASSOCIATION

22100 Gratiot Avenue

Eastpointe, MI 48021-2227

800-598-4668

586-776-3900

Fax: 586-776-3903

http://www.aarda.org

Email: aarda@aarda.org

CENTERS FOR MEDICARE AND MEDICAID SERVICES

http://www.cms.gov/

MEDICARE
http://www.medicare.gov/

CENTERS FOR DISEASE CONTROL AND PREVENTION, DISABILITY AND HEALTH ISSUES, INFORMATION FOR CAREGIVERS
Centers for Disease Control and Prevention National Center on Birth Defects and Developmental Disabilities Division of Human Development and Disability
1600 Clifton Road
MS E-88
Atlanta, GA 30333
800-CDC-INFO (800-232-4636
TTY: 888-232-6348

ANGEL FLIGHT, INC.
1515 East 71st Street, Ste. 312
Tulsa, OK 74136
918-749-8992
http://www.angelflight.com
Email: angel@angelflight.Com

HOUSTON GROUND ANGELS
http://houstongroundangels.org

DYNAVOXTECH
DynaVox Mayer-Johnson
2100 Wharton Street, Ste. 400
Pittsburgh, PA 15203
866-DYNAVOX (396-2869)
(412) 381-4883
(412) 381-5241
www. Dynavoxtech .com/

CLEARINGHOUSE ON DISABILITY INFORMATION
Special Education & Rehabilitative Services Communications & Customer Service Team
550 12th Street, SW Rm. 5133
Washington, DC 20202-2550
202-245-7307
202-205-5637 (TTD)
http://www.ed.Gov/about/offices/list/osers

VETERANS AFFAIRS FAMILY CAREGIVER SUPPORT

Benefits: 1-800-827-1000

Health Care: 1-877-222-VETS (8387)

Veterans Crisis Line: 1-800-273-8255 Press 1
http://www.caregiver.va.gov/

ADAPTIVE EQUIPMENT FUNDING RESOURCES FOR SPECIAL NEEDS & ADAPTIVE EQUIPMENT
http://www.especialneeds.com/funding-resources-special-needs-adaptive-hequipment.html
http://www.especialneeds.com/adaptive-products.html

PATIENT ADVOCATE FOUNDATION

421 Butler Farm Road

Hampton, VA 23666

Ph: 800-532-5274

Fax: 757-873-8999
www.patientadvocate.org
help@patientadvocate.org

NATIONAL INSTITUTES OF HEALTH

Vast clearinghouse of information and resources
http://www.nih.gov/

NATIONAL ORGANIZATION FOR RARE DISORDERS

PH: 203-744-0100
www.rarediseases.org

CPSIA information can be obtained at www.ICGtesting.com
Printed in the USA
LVOW01s1252260915

455844LV00001B/2/P